Mary and the Divine Sophia:

The Salvation of Universal Wisdom

RON MACFARLANE

Copyright © 2016 Ron MacFarlane

All rights reserved.

Published 2016 by
Greater Mysteries Publications
Mission, BC, Canada

Cover Design: Ron MacFarlane

Printed in the United States of America

ISBN:
ISBN-13: 978-0994007780
ISBN-10: 0994007787

DEDICATION

This work is lovingly dedicated to our sister-in-Christ and world mother, Blessed Mary, who is the first of our humanity to be bodily assumed into heaven following the resurrection of Our Saviour. Immense gratitude is also acknowledged for Mary's courageous opposition to evil, and for her compassionate maternal care as the foremost representative of the Holy Mother-Spirit for all mankind.

CONTENTS

Introduction   i

Chapter 1 An Historical Background to Understanding Sophia
- 1.1 Sophia as Defined in Ancient Greece and in Pre-Christian Gnosticism   1
- 1.2 Sophia as Transformed by Post-Christian Gnosticism   2
- 1.3 The Logos-Word versus Holy Sophia   3
- 1.4 Is Sophia Indicated in the Hebrew Old Testament?   5
- 1.5 The Hebrew Sophia: Spirit-Being or Figurative Speech?   6

Chapter 2 Wisdom (Sophia) as a Fundamental Requirement of Personhood
- 2.1 The Feminization and Personification of Ancient Wisdom   9
- 2.2 The Existential Superiority of Personhood   10
- 2.3 What are the Fundamental Characteristics and Essential Requirements of Personhood?   11
- 2.4 Personhood and Wisdom (Sophia)   12
- 2.5 Psychologically Understanding the Concise Declaration of Existence—"I am"   12

Chapter 3 The Divine Feminine-Person of the Holy Trinity
- 3.1 Using the Knowledge of Human Personhood to Understand Divine Personhood   15
- 3.2 Esoterically Understanding the Threefold Nature of the Supreme Personhood of God   16
- 3.3 Understanding the Mystery of Divine Gender   18

3.4	The Divine Trinity According to Esoteric-Christianity	19
3.5	The Role and Function of the Heavenly Father and the Holy Mother	20
3.6	The Divine Trinity as a Personal Relationship of Love	21

Chapter 4 The Holy Spirit (Mother) as the True Divine Sophia

4.1	The Divine Trinity as Will, Wisdom and United Love	23
4.2	The Holy Mother as the Divine Sophia	25
4.3	The Holy Mother as the "Substance" of the Divine Nature	27
4.4	The Holy Spirit (Mother) as the Ultimate Source of All Universal Matter	27

Chapter 5 Universal Wisdom as the Cosmic Reflection of the Divine Sophia

5.1	The Universe as a Living, Sentient Macrocosmic Being	29
5.2	The Logos-Word as the Divine Self-Concept	30
5.3	The Divine Self-Concept of the Logos-Word and the Divine Self-Consciousness of the Eternal Son	31
5.4	The Trinitarian Reflection of the Logos-Word	32
5.5	Universal Wisdom (Sophia) as an Essential Attribute of the Logos-Word	33

Chapter 6 Historical Manifestations of Universal Wisdom-Sophia

6.1	The Background Mythology of the Egyptian Goddess, Isis	35
6.2	Interpreting the Mythological Symbolism of Isis-Sophia	37
6.3	The Pre-Christian Symbolism of Mother Isis and the Child Horus	38
6.4	Esoterically Understanding Philo-Sophia	40
6.5	"Lady Philosophy" in the Sixth-Century Literature of Boethius	42
6.6	"Lady Philosophy" in the Thirteenth-Century Love Poetry of Dante	43

Chapter 7 The Luciferic Distortion of Wisdom-Sophia: The New Isis-Myth

7.1	The Unreliability of Human Intellection	47
7.2	The Beginning of Luciferic Interference in Human Evolution	48
7.3	The Luciferic Corruption of Intellectual Truth	49
7.4	A Modern-Day Isis-Myth of Human Cognition	50
7.5	Christ-Jesus and the Divine Rescue of Cosmic Truth (Isis-Sophia)	51
7.6	Gnosticism as a Luciferic Distortion of Cosmic Truth	53

Chapter 8 Ahrimanic Materialism and the Birth of Anthropo-Sophia

8.1	The Rapid Rise of Ahrimanic Materialism in the Modern Age	55
8.2	Nineteenth-Century Materialism and the Ahrimanic War in Heaven	56
8.3	St. Michael's Descent to the Earth and the Formation of Spiritual Science	57
8.4	The Birth of Anthropo-Sophia: The "Wisdom of Mankind"	58
8.5	Correctly Understanding the "Being" of Anthropo-Sophia	59

Chapter 9 The Different Jesus-Families in St. Luke and St. Matthew

9.1	Mary, the Mother of Jesus, as an Important Figure in World History	63
9.2	Reading the Akashic Records to Clairvoyantly Study and Understand the Past	64
9.3	The Historical Co-Existence of Two Different Jesus Families	65
9.4	Different Family Accounts in the Gospel of St. Matthew and the Gospel of St. Luke	67

Chapter 10 The "Blessed Virgin Mary" of St. Luke's Gospel

10.1	The "Heavenly-Adam and the "Heavenly-Eve"	69
10.2	St. Luke's Mary: A "Virginal" Soul Without Previous Incarnations	71
10.3	St. Luke's Jesus-Child: The Incarnation of the "Heavenly-Adam"	72

10.4	The Predestined, Premature Death of St. Luke's Mary	75
10.5	The After-Death Existence of St. Luke's Mary as the "Blessed Virgin Mary"	76

Chapter 11 St. Matthew's Mary: The "Mother of the World"

11.1	The "Earthly-Adam" and the "Earthly Eve"	79
11.2	St. Matthew's Mary: The Incarnation of the Earthly-Eve	80
11.3	St. Matthew's Jesus-Child: The Incarnation of the Bodhisattva-Zarathustra	81
11.4	The Predestined, Premature Death of St. Matthew's Jesus-Boy	83
11.5	The Two Jesus-Families of Nazareth Become One	84
11.6	The Profound Inner Transformations of St. Matthew's Mary	84
11.7	The After-Death Existence of St. Matthew's Mary as "Blessed Mary, the Mother of the World"	87

Chapter 12 Myths and Misconception About Wisdom-Sophia

12.1	The Heavenly-Sophia is not the Same as the Divine Sophia	91
12.2	There is no Such Thing as the "Triple Goddess"	92
12.3	The Blessed Virgin Mary is not Anthropo-Sophia	93
12.4	Sophia is not the Feminine Counterpart to Christ	97
12.5	The Coming "Age of Sophia" is a Luciferic Distraction	99
12.6	The "Virgin Sophia" is not Simply the Purified Consciousness Soul	101
12.7	The Gospel of St. John is not Literally the "Virgin Sophia"	104

Conclusion	107
Notes	109
Select Bibliography	117
Other Books	119

MARY
AND THE
DIVINE SOPHIA

INTRODUCTION

NO DOUBT, anyone interested in Christian esotericism will have noticed that there is a widespread modern-day revival of interest in the ancient gnostic concept of "Sophia" amongst a strange diversity of groups: wiccans, neo-pagans, New Agers, neo-gnostics, Catholic mystics, Orthodox Christians, radical feminists, and anthroposophists. Adding to this ideological mélange is the exotic variety of Sophia designations and conceptions: the Divine Sophia, the heavenly-sophia, the earthly-sophia, Hagia Sophia, the goddess Sophia, the Aeon Sophia, the Virgin Sophia, Sophia-Achamoth, Pistis Sophia, Isis-Sophia, Jesus Sophia, theo-sophia, philo-sophia and anthropo-sophia.

Not surprisingly, then, this cacophony of Sophias is very often contradictory, confusing, distorted, invented, erroneous, and (sadly) rarely enlightening. It is not difficult to detect that "esoteric entrepreneurs" have seized this current "thirst for Sophia" to offer up a potpourri of books, courses, conferences, workshops, lessons, websites, video clips, internet articles—even worship services—to inundate, titillate and financially captivate any novice Sophia seeker.

So, what is a sincere Christian esotericist to make of this fervent Sophia phenomenon: "Is it a positive and healthy spiritual development, or is it a regressive and outmoded religious diversion?" This particular discourse—*Mary and the*

INTRODUCTION

Divine Sophia—delves deeply and genuinely into this important question in order to establish spiritual fact from unspiritual fiction.

In order to adequately answer this question, however, profound esoteric investigation into the Trinitarian nature of God, as well as the universal being of the Logos-Word, together with the fundamental underlying principles of the created cosmos will need to be detailed and discussed. Some of this previously-guarded esoteric information may be quite new and unfamiliar to many readers; but every effort has been made to present it in clear, understandable concepts.

Furthermore, since the mother of Jesus is very often intimately associated or connected to historical and present-day conceptions of Sophia, a comprehensive study will also be undertaken regarding Mary and her special relationship to the Divine Sophia; relying heavily on the spiritual-scientific research of Austrian philosopher and esotericist, Rudolf Steiner (1861–1925). Once again, a great deal of this information will be startlingly new to those unfamiliar with anthroposophy; but, as before, great care has been taken to present this possibly-unfamiliar information in a comprehensible, intellectually-accessible way.

It is sincerely intended that this discourse will provide the earnest esotericist with reliable, trustworthy and objective spiritual knowledge in order to confidently know and understand the mystery-truth of the heavenly-sophia; and thereby extricate her from the distortions and falsifications of Lucifer and Ahriman.

CHAPTER 1

AN HISTORICAL BACKGROUND TO UNDERSTANDING SOPHIA

1.1 Sophia as Defined in Ancient Greece and in Pre-Christian Gnosticism

IN CONTRAST TO today's confusing conceptual usage, the word "sophia" began simply as an ancient Greek designation for "wisdom." The word "philosophy" is derived from philo (love) and sophia (wisdom). Philosophy, then, literally means "the love of wisdom." Likewise, the word "theosophy" is derived from theos (God) and sophia (wisdom); literally meaning "the wisdom of God."

To Classical Greek philosopher Plato (c.427 BC–c.347 BC), sophia-wisdom was one of the four cardinal virtues of the soul, together with temperance, courage and justice. Not surprisingly as well, Greek mythology also attributed the virtue of sophia-wisdom to a particular goddess, Athena Parthenos ("Virgin Athena").

The idea that sophia-wisdom was more than simply a soul virtue possessed by humans and deities; but was instead, an actual spiritual being—a divine goddess of wisdom—really began with ancient Gnosticism: an exotically-diverse and widespread syncretic religious movement that began in the centuries just prior to Christ. Gnosticism claimed that salvation could be achieved through the acquisition and application of *secret* knowledge ("gnosis"), and that *higher* wisdom was personified in a feminine celestial being (an "aeon") known as Sophia.

According to pre-Christian gnostic belief, aeons such as Sophia were created in complementary pairs ("syzygies"). Unfortunately, Sophia committed a serious spiritual transgression by birthing a lesser being (through emanation) without the consent and cooperation of her aeon-consort. As a result, Sophia tragically fell from her originally-glorious high estate; and her illicit offspring was born a flawed and inferior being (known as "the Demiurge" or "Ialdabaoth") who went on to create our depraved and degenerate universe with degraded and corrupted material.

In her fallen position, Sophia stood midway between the light-filled heavens above (the "Pleroma") and the dark, evil universe (wherein humanity existed) below. In a gnostic sense, then, Sophia was the "mother of the material world."

1.2   Sophia as Transformed by Post-Christian Gnosticism

Gnosticism continued to decreasingly survive for a few brief centuries into the Christian era. Predictably during that time, it eclectically incorporated a number of Christian ideas, figures and stories into its phantasmagoric ideology. A colourful example of Christian incorporation is contained in the famous gnostic writing, *Pistis Sophia*, written sometime between 200 and 300 AD.

In the *Pistis Sophia*, Christ gnostically became the aeon

consort of Sophia. After Sophia's fall from grace and the consequent creation of the material world, Christ undertakes a mission to rescue her from the chaotic darkness below. As partially described in the text:

> "And at the commandment of my Father, the First Mystery which looketh within, I myself went down into the chaos ... And I took away the power of all the emanations of Self-willed, and they all fell down in the chaos powerless. And I led forth Pistis Sophia, she being on the right of Gabriēl and Michaēl. And the great light-stream entered again into her ... And I led Pistis Sophia forth from the chaos, she treading underfoot the serpent-faced emanation of Self-willed, and moreover treading underfoot the seven-faced-basilisk emanation, and treading underfoot the lion- and dragon-faced power."

Most of this fancifully-gnosticized Christianity was understandably considered far too heretical, and thereby soundly rejected, by the early Church. Remarkably, however, a morphisized and safely-diluted version of the gnostic Sophia was embraced by many Church Fathers, and even lastingly incorporated into Orthodox Christian belief. In the acceptably-altered version, Sophia was equated with the second Person of the Trinity—God the Son—in a manner similar to the Word and the Son. But in this case (to paraphrase St. John):

> In the beginning was Sophia, the holy wisdom. She was with God in the beginning; and nothing in the world was created without her. In order to redeem mankind, the holy Sophia took flesh on earth as Christ-Jesus; but the world recognized and understood her not.

1.3 The Logos-Word versus Holy Sophia

AN HISTORICAL BACKGROUND TO UNDERSTANDING SOPHIA

Ancient Greek philosophy, beginning with Heraclitus (c.535–c.475 BC), postulated that there was a universal principle of reason and intelligence (wisdom)—called the "logos"—which fundamentally pervaded the entire sense-perceptible world, and which gave it order and meaning. St. John later referred to the logos at the beginning of his Gospel (written between 90 and 110 AD); but in that case, the term was deified and Christianized to mean the wisdom of God that is personified in the Son. Despite its deep and complex meaning in John's Gospel, the Logos has been translated in English simply as, the "Word," as indicated in the following:

> In the beginning was the [Logos] Word, and the Word was with God, and the Word was God. He was in the beginning with God; all things were made through him, and without him was not anything made that was made. In him was life, and the life was the light of men … And the Word became flesh and dwelt among us, full of grace and truth; we have beheld his glory, glory as of the only Son from the Father. (Jn 1:1–14)

Since St. John's Christianized Greek concept of the Logos-Word was very similar to the Christianized gnostic concept of Hagia Sophia (Holy Wisdom), the Logos-Word very soon became the preferred religious choice between the two—particularly with Western Catholic Christianity. In Eastern Orthodox Christianity, however, the worship of Hagia Sophia continued in small measure, particularly in the Russian Church.

No doubt, the climax of sophianic Christian worship was the sixth-century construction of the magnificent basilica of Hagia Sophia in Constantinople by Byzantine Emperor Justinian I. This famed basilica served as the centre of the Eastern Orthodox Church for nearly a thousand years, until Constantinople was captured by the Ottoman Turks in 1453, who then converted the basilica into an imperial mosque.

Nevertheless, in Russia there continues to be numerous churches dedicated to Holy Sophia, as well as two surviving cathedrals: the eleventh-century cathedral of Divine Sophia in Kiev, and the eleventh-century cathedral of Holy Sophia in Novgorod.

1.4   Is Sophia Indicated in the Hebrew Old Testament?

The Old Testament, as initially compiled by the Catholic Church, contains 46 books; 39 of which were originally written in Hebrew, and 7 of which were originally written in Greek. These seven books: Tobit, Judith, Wisdom, Sirach, Baruch, and First and Second Maccabees are known as the "deuterocanonicals." For some strange reason, these particular scriptural writings were not recognized by the early Protestants, even though they were embraced by Christ-Jesus and the apostles.

When looking for any Old Testament references to sophia, since it is a Greek term, there is predictably no mention in the 39 Hebrew-written books. In Hebrew, the word for wisdom is "chokmah," not sophia. In the Greek-written deuterocanonical books, however, sophia is predictably used numerous times as a term for wisdom.

Interestingly, in a manner similar to Gnosticism, sophia-wisdom is depicted as an exalted spiritual female figure in the books of Wisdom and Sirach. For example:

> Wisdom [Sophia] is radiant and unfading, and she is easily discerned by those who love her, and is found by those who seek her ... To fix one's thought on her is perfect understanding ... The beginning of wisdom is the most sincere desire for instruction, and concern for instruction is love of her, and love of her is the keeping of her laws, and giving heed to her laws is assurance of immortality, and immortality brings one near to God. (Wis 6:12–19)

AN HISTORICAL BACKGROUND TO UNDERSTANDING SOPHIA

I called upon God, and the spirit of wisdom [sophia] came to me. I preferred her to scepters and thrones ... I loved her more than health and beauty, and I chose to have her rather than light, because her radiance never ceases ... For in her there is a spirit that is intelligent, holy, unique, manifold, subtle, mobile, clear, unpolluted, distinct, invulnerable, loving the good, keen, irresistible, beneficent, humane, steadfast, sure, free from anxiety, all-powerful, overseeing all, and penetrating through all spirits that are intelligent and pure and most subtle ... because of her pureness she pervades and penetrates all things. For she is a breath of the power of God, and a pure emanation of the glory of the Almighty; therefore nothing defiled gains entrance into her. For she is a reflection of eternal light, a spotless mirror of the working of God, and an image of his goodness ... For she is more beautiful than the sun, and excels every constellation of the stars. Compared with the light she is found to be superior, for it is succeeded by the night, but against wisdom evil does not prevail. (Wis 7:7–30)

All wisdom [sophia] comes from the Lord and is with him forever ... Wisdom was created before all things ... The Lord himself created wisdom; he saw her and apportioned her, he poured her out upon all his works. She dwells with all flesh according to his gift, and he supplied her to those who love him ... The fear of the Lord is the crown of wisdom, making peace and perfect health to flourish. He saw her and apportioned her; he rained down knowledge and discerning comprehension, and he exalted the glory of those who held her fast. (Sir 1:1–19)

1.5 The Hebrew Sophia: Spirit-Being or Figurative Speech?

Given the recognized fact that Old Testament Judaism was strictly monotheistic, it is totally unlikely that sophia-wisdom as described in Wisdom and Sirach was an actual deific-being. Even though ancient Judaism certainly recognized spirit-beings such as angels, archangels, seraphim and cherubim, these were beings created by God; and not self-existent gods and goddesses, or divine emanations like the gnostic Sophia.

Moreover, when the word "sophia" was used in the Old Testament to denote wisdom, it was not capitalized as a proper name like the gnostic Sophia. Since specific spirit-beings *are* properly named in the Old Testament—such as Michael, Gabriel and Raphael—no doubt if the Hebrew sophia was referring to an actual spirit-being, it would have been capitalized.

Clearly when ancient Hebrew scripture referred to wisdom (sophia) as the feminine "she" and "her," this was just figurative speech: inanimate wisdom had simply been poetically personified. Furthermore, this was hardly unusual since figurative language and personification were commonly used throughout the Old Testament. Most of the creation story in Genesis, for example, was conveyed in figurative language.

To mention a couple of instances of personification in Genesis, there is of course the "fast-talking" serpent in the garden of Eden; and when Cain killed Abel, the "voice" of his brother's blood "cried out" to the Lord from the ground (Gen 4:10).

Even though the personification of wisdom (sophia) in the Old Testament was not particularly unusual, what is esoterically noteworthy and highly significant is the fact that wisdom had been personified *in the feminine*—as a female quality. Was this simply an arbitrary literary choice; or is there a deeper spiritual reason that wisdom was considered to be feminine by Hebrews, Gnostics, Greeks, Romans and

Orthodox Christians alike?

CHAPTER 2

WISDOM (SOPHIA) AS A FUNDAMENTAL REQUIREMENT OF PERSONHOOD

2.1 The Feminization and Personification of Ancient Wisdom

RATHER INTERESTINGLY, about one quarter of the world's languages incorporate a system of "grammatical gender," where nouns are classified according to masculine, feminine, neuter, animate or inanimate distinctions. These classifications are usually determined by biological sex, humanness, animacy, morphology (basic structure) or phonology (sound formation). And in some instances, the gender determination appears to be entirely random.

In the case of wisdom—an inanimate mental attribute—how is it that this particular word was regarded as a feminine gender noun in ancient Hebrew ("chokmah"), Greek ("sophia") and Latin ("sapientia")? It's unlikely that wisdom became a feminine noun on the basis that women in ancient society were viewed as having more wisdom than men, since the wisdom of King Solomon was unequalled in

Hebrew history; and almost all the philosophers in ancient Greece and Rome were men.

Perhaps it was this historical fact that many powerful and influential *men* in ancient times were "lovers of wisdom" (philosophers)—who longed-for and adored wisdom as a precious and valuable pursuit—which explains why this inanimate mental capacity became a feminine noun. Perhaps wisdom was feminine to ancient male thinkers in the same way that the sea was feminine to seasoned male sailors—"their life, their love and their lady."

In any case, once wisdom was established as a feminine noun in several of the ancient languages, it would then be quite easy (and perhaps predictable) to personify the word by using the gender agreements "she" and "her."

While the foregoing conjectures clearly demonstrate that clever explanations can be easily generated intellectually, to esoteric-Christian understanding, there are far-deeper and much more profound reasons why ancient wisdom was feminized and personified.

2.2 The Existential Superiority of Personhood

In order to truly understand why wisdom has been feminized and personified in ancient (and in modern) times, it is necessary to gain a basic understanding of the characteristics and essentials of "personhood"—what constitutes the existence of a "person" in general, and a human "person" in particular. By doing so, a deeper understanding will be gained of the threefold personhood of God. Further examining the greater mysteries of the Trinitarian nature of God—how and why the One Life is in essence a perfect unity of three divine-persons—will reveal the transcendent reason why wisdom-sophia, at the highest levels, is in reality a "divine feminine-person."

Beginning then with an examination of personhood, as insightfully expressed by German philosopher and Catholic theologian, Dietrich von Hildebrand (1889–1977), in *Transformation in Christ: On the Christian Attitude* (2001): "[A]ny personal being is in essence superior to everything impersonal." Stated even more succinctly: "A person is always superior to a thing."

What should be an obvious self-evident truth has, in modern times, become obscured and distorted under ideological layers of scientific materialism: the erroneous belief that everything in the perceptible universe is simply the result of random chemical activity. Since persons are superior to things, human beings can never be the result of random chemical activity. Moreover, since an effect cannot logically be greater than its cause, a person cannot logically be the superior product of inferior chemical causation.

So if persons are not derived from any chemical causes in the known physical-material universe, from whence do they occur? The only logical answer is from a superphysical-spiritual source. Esoterically analogous to the scientific assertion that the entire physical universe of matter, energy, space and time derives from a primordial cosmic singularity, esoteric science similarly maintains that all persons (heavenly and human) derive from a singular, superphysical Person who is infinite and eternal.

2.3 What are the Fundamental Characteristics and Essential Requirements of Personhood?

In order for any life-form within the created universe to qualify for personhood, it must possess three essential fundamentals. Personhood does not exist if any one of these three fundamentals is lacking. Firstly, the life-form must possess a distinct self-identity, an individual ego. Secondly, it must possess conscious awareness; there must be the innate capacity to know and to understand. Thirdly, the life-form must possess self-consciousness; that is, the conscious awareness of its own ego-self. Phrased another way, every person is essentially comprised of (1) being, (2) knowing, and (3) self-awareness.[1]

Careful observers may have noticed that two of the three fundamentals of personhood are primary and antecedent to the subsequent third. Obviously a person must possess (1) an ego-self, and (2) conscious awareness *before* they can exhibit (3) self-conscious awareness. In psychological fact, then, self-consciousness is the combination—or union—of self and consciousness, or being and knowing. Or expressed in more "familial" language, self-consciousness is the generated "offspring" of the two "parent" fundamentals of ego-being and conscious-knowing.

2.4 Personhood and Wisdom (Sophia)

The word, "wisdom," can also be synonymously used for "conscious knowing" or "sentient understanding." In other words, when describing the three fundamentals of personhood, it is just as accurate to say that they are: (1) self-identity, (2) wisdom-knowing, and (3) self-conscious awareness. Wisdom-sophia, then, is a fundamental requirement of personhood. However, at the level of human personhood, wisdom-sophia can hardly be described as a deific feminine personification. So if there is any reality to the notion that "Sophia" is an actual feminine-being (person), it is obviously necessary to look beyond human existence for a satisfactory answer.

2.5 Psychologically Understanding the Concise Declaration of Existence—"I am"

As a consequence of possessing self-conscious awareness, human persons can declare, "I am," as a meaningful declaration of their own self-existence. While the superficial thinkers of today rarely examine and appreciate this cogent assertion, it nevertheless has deep and profound meaning. To begin with, "I am" is a mental conception—a word construct—that represents or mirrors self-consciousness. And mirroring the dual components of self-consciousness, "I am" is comprised of two distinct words: (1) "I" which represents the ego-self (or being), and (2) "am" which represents conscious awareness (or knowing). The word "am," in this context, is the shortened expression for "*am* consciously aware that I exist."

United together, the separate word-concepts, "I" and "am" become a potent word-symbol—a *logo*—for self-consciousness, for ego-awareness.[2] It's also important at this point to clearly understand that "I am" is a *word-symbol* for self-consciousness; it is not the actual first-hand *experience* of self-consciousness.

By better understanding the nature of personhood in general and human personhood in particular, we now have a firmer foundation on which to comprehend the Supreme Person of God, and why wisdom-sophia is much more than simply a "thing," but also a "divine feminine-person."

CHAPTER 3

THE DIVINE FEMININE-PERSON OF THE HOLY TRINITY

3.1 Using the Knowledge of Human Personhood to Understand Divine Personhood

AS PREVIOUSLY EMPHASIZED in Chapter 2: "a person is always superior to a thing." God, therefore, as the ultimate source and creator of all that is, cannot be a thing—such as an all-pervading life-energy (like a "Star Wars" force); or an underlying universal intelligence (as professed in "deism"). Moreover, since the ultimate reality must logically be infinite and eternal, the Person of God must be infinite and eternal; in truth, a "Super-Person."

Unlike the divine Person, human persons have a beginning. But since God must logically be indivisible, how is it that the one supreme Person can create a multitude of finite persons without division, separation, detachment or partition? Moreover, since God cannot perform the logically impossible—such as create another God—how can he create human persons without illogically reproducing himself?

The biblical book of Genesis has for centuries provided the obvious answer (for those willing to see): "So God created man in his own image, in the image of God he created him; male and female he created them" (Gen 1:27). In other words, God created other persons by making mirror-images—true reflections—of himself. Human persons, then, are not chance accumulations of lifeless chemicals in an insensate physical universe; but are instead, living mirrored likenesses of a superphysical, totally-alive God-Person.

Even though a mirrored image is not the actual subject-reality being reflected, it is nevertheless a true representation. As such, accurate knowledge of the reflected subject can be reliably obtained by carefully examining the mirrored-reflection.

3.2 Esoterically Understanding the Threefold Nature of the Supreme Personhood of God

As a mirrored reflection of the singular God-Person, the threefold nature of the human person—being, knowing and self-awareness—has its existential origin in the divine nature. Though the divine nature is also fundamentally threefold, it is raised to a far-transcendent level of reality since divine nature is logically infinite, eternal, unsurpassed and perfect in every attribute. Within the divine nature, then, the transcendent equivalent of the human ego-self is " omnipotent total-being"; the transcendent equivalent of human conscious-knowing is "omniscient all-consciousness"; and the transcendent equivalent of human self-consciousness is "supernal self-awareness" (please refer to Figure 1 on the following page for a diagrammatical representation of the Supreme Personhood of God).

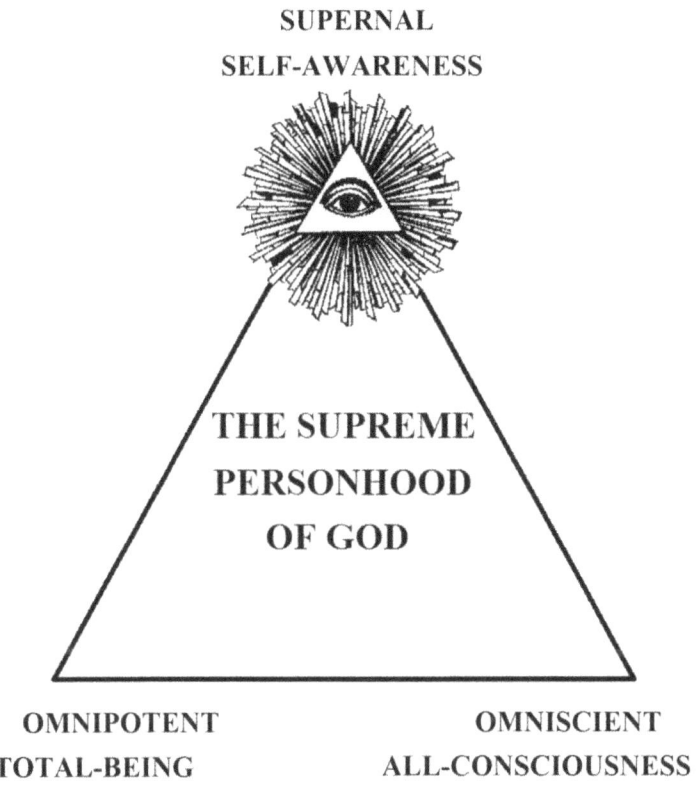

Figure 1: The Supreme Personhood of God

Moreover, since the divine nature is alive and existent to an infinite and perfect degree, from our limited human experience, God is not simply "real"; but in truth, "totally-real," "hyper-real" or "super-real." Within this divine hyper-reality, the three distinct fundamental essentials of personhood—being, knowing and self-awareness—are instilled and infused with such transcendent life that they become livingly personified. Amazing as this is to human comprehension, the three fundamentals of divine personhood are not "divine-things"; but are themselves "distinct divine-entities."

In other words, " omnipotent total-being" is not a divine-thing, but a personified divine-entity. Likewise, "omniscient all-consciousness" is a personified divine-entity; as is "supernal self-awareness." Furthermore, since these three divine-entities are in perfect union with each other, they can also be correctly regarded as "divine-persons." This is not to say, of course, that there are three separate Gods in existence; but rather, the one super-personhood of God is a perfect unity of three essential divine-persons.[3]

3.3 Understanding the Mystery of Divine Gender

As esoterically indicated in Genesis, when God created human beings in his own mirror-image and reflected-likeness: "male and female he created them" (Gen 1:27). Correctly understood, this scriptural truth clearly indicates that there is a masculine and a feminine aspect to the divine nature.

Naturally one must be reverentially careful when applying human terms to the divine nature; and this, of course, includes human gender distinctions. Obviously, the divine nature is transcendently more than simply "male" and/or "female." Nevertheless, what is limitedly reflected in human nature as "masculine" and "feminine" have their ultimate source in the infinite and eternal nature of God. Within the divine nature, then, the qualities and characteristics of masculinity and femininity are transcendently raised to the level of infinite and eternal perfection.

According to esoteric-Christian understanding, deific masculinity is polarized in one of the three divine-persons—the divine-person of omnipotent total-being. Deific femininity, however, is polarized in the divine-person of omniscient all-consciousness. Since self-consciousness is a union of being and knowing, the divine-person of supernal self-awareness is a perfect union of deific masculinity and deific femininity.

In accordance with the gender distinctions of the divine nature, esoteric-Christianity also refers to the three divine-persons in more personal, familial terms. The masculine divine-person of omnipotent total-being is esoterically referred to as the "Heavenly Father." The feminine divine-person of omniscient all-consciousness is esoterically referred to as the "Holy Mother." And the dual-gendered divine-person of supernal self-awareness is esoterically referred to as the "Eternal Son."[4]

3.4 The Divine Trinity According to Esoteric-Christianity

The Heavenly Father, the Holy Mother and the Eternal Son constitute what is understood in esoteric-Christianity as the "Divine Trinity." This understanding differs somewhat from the "Blessed Trinity" of Western theology, which is comprised of the Father, the Son and the Holy Spirit. To many early Christians, however, the Holy Spirit was regarded as feminine, since the ancient Hebrew word for spirit was "ruach"—a feminine-gendered noun. For instance, St. Jerome (347–420), who translated the Bible from Hebrew and Greek into Latin (the Vulgate), expressed the following:

> In the Gospel of the Hebrews that the Nazarenes read it says, "Just now my mother, the Holy Spirit, took me." Now no one should be offended by this, because 'spirit' in Hebrew is feminine, while in our [Latin] language it is masculine and in the Greek it is neuter. In divinity, however, there is no gender. (*Jerome's Commentary on Isaiah II*)

Also, second-century Church leader, Clement of Alexandria (c.150–c.215), similarly wrote:

> And God Himself is love; and out of love to us became feminine. In His ineffable essence He is Father; in His compassion to us He became Mother. The Father by loving became feminine: and the great proof of this is He whom He begot of Himself [the Son]: and the fruit brought forth by love is love. (*Who is the Rich Man that Shall be Saved*; Chap. 37)

To esoteric-Christianity, then, the Holy Spirit is equated with the Holy Mother, and is consequently also referred to as the "Holy Mother-Spirit."

3.5 The Role and Function of the Heavenly Father and the Holy Mother

Within the divine nature, the role and function of the Heavenly Father and the Holy Mother are mutually obverse and complementary. The Heavenly Father performs the masculine function of singularization; that is, of contracting the divine nature to a central point of being. The Holy Mother performs the complementary feminine function of diversification; that is, of expanding the divine nature to a peripheral expanse of knowing. The back-and-forth, rhythmic interplay between the centralizing activity of the Heavenly Father and the proliferating activity of the Holy Mother generates the harmoniously balanced unity of supernal self-awareness that is personified in the Eternal Son.[5]

Even though the Heavenly Father and the Holy Mother have existed throughout eternity, and therefore have no beginning, the masculine function of the Heavenly Father can also be correctly understood to be an "initiating" or "inseminating" impulse within the divine nature. The

Heavenly Father's concentrated, singular point of total-being acts as a seed-impulse which stimulates and excites the expansive, germinating, all-knowing feminine activity of the Holy Mother. The rhythmic and harmonious interplay between the Heavenly Father and the Holy Mother "eternally generates" the divine-person of the Eternal Son.[6]

3.6 The Divine Trinity as a Personal Relationship of Love

When St. John the Evangelist succinctly declared: "God is love" (1 Jn 4:16), he was not simply stating that love is a virtue or attribute of God; but much more profoundly, that love is the true essence of the divine nature. In other words, divine love is the fundamental reality of who God is.

Applying this transcendent truth to the divine Trinity, then, the Heavenly Father can be regarded as the perfect personification of paternal love; the Holy Mother can be regarded as the perfect personification of maternal love; and the Eternal Son can be regarded as the perfect personification of the mutual love between the Heavenly Father and the Holy Mother.

The eternal rhythmic interplay between the Heavenly Father and the Holy Mother is, therefore, much more than simply a mechanical-style oscillation or an automatic vibratory motion; but instead, a pulsating expression of infinite mutual love. In actuality, then, the love between the heavenly Father and the Holy Mother is so real, so deep and so powerful, that a third divine-person—the Eternal Son—is eternally generated from their consummate union.[7]

CHAPTER 4

THE HOLY SPIRIT (MOTHER) AS THE TRUE DIVINE SOPHIA

4.1 The Divine Trinity as Will, Wisdom and United Love

TO CONTINUE WHAT has been esoterically examined in Chapter 3, the masculine function of the Heavenly Father provides the initiating spark of motion and activity within the divine nature. This ignites the feminine function of the Holy Mother to expand and multiply the activating seed-impulse. The proliferating expansion of the Holy Mother, however, does not continue indefinitely; but reaches a periphery of enervation, whereupon the centripetal activity of the Heavenly Father draws the divine nature back to a singular point of concentrated being. Likewise, the contractive activity of the Heavenly Father does not continue indefinitely; but at a specific degree of compressed intensity the masculine spark of supernal activation is re-ignited, and the feminine function of the Holy Mother is re-engaged, thereby continuing the rhythmic motion of the divine nature that has occurred throughout eternity.

From this brief summation, it's quite clear that the masculine function of the Heavenly Father and the feminine function of the Holy Mother are *both* necessary within the divine nature in order to maintain a perfect balance of harmonious activity—which is personified in the Eternal Son.

Since the Heavenly Father eternally provides the initiating impulse of divine motion, he is esoterically understood to embody the omnipotent *force* of divine will. In other words, the divine will is perfectly actualized in the Heavenly Father. Furthermore, since the Holy Mother eternally provides the proliferating impulse of divine motion, she is esoterically understood to embody the omniscient *substance* of divine all-knowing. Omniscient all-knowing can also be referred to as "divine wisdom." In other words, divine wisdom is perfectly actualized in the Holy Mother.

Keeping in mind that the true nature of God is divine love, the Heavenly Father can also be understood to be the personification of the "will of divine love." Likewise, the Holy Mother can also be understood to be the personification of the "wisdom of divine love." Moreover, since the Eternal Son is the perfect union of the paternal love of the Heavenly Father and the maternal love of the Holy Mother, he can also be understood to be the personification of the "unity of divine love." And since this unity of divine love generates supernal self-awareness, the Eternal Son additionally personifies the "self-awareness of divine love" (for a diagrammatic representation of the Divine Trinity, please refer to Figure 2 on the following page).

In keeping with the teachings of Western theology, it's important to understand at this point that even though the three divine-persons of the Trinity personify distinct functions and essentials of the divine nature, because they are so perfectly united in the supreme personhood of God, they are co-existent, co-equal and consubstantial. As amazing as this seems to the human mind, while each divine-person is existentially distinct, they also totally and completely share in the function, activity and personification of the others.

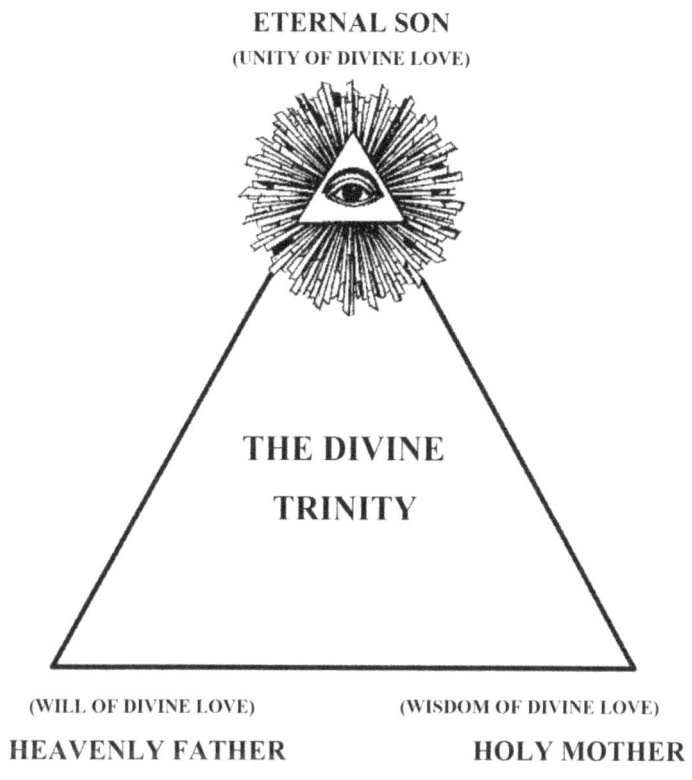

Figure 2: The Divine Trinity of Will, Wisdom and Unified Love

4.2 The Holy Mother as the Divine Sophia

Since divine wisdom is perfectly actualized in the Holy Mother, the Holy Mother can be esoterically termed the "divine personification of wisdom-sophia" or more simply as the "Divine Sophia." According to esoteric-Christianity, then, the feminization and personification of divine wisdom by the ancient Hebrews, Greeks, Romans, Gnostics and Orthodox Christians was not simply poetic fancy, figurative speech or grammatical genderization; but was intuitively based on deep spiritual truth.

But to be esoterically clear, the Divine Sophia exists as a divine-person within the Trinitarian nature of the One God. The Divine Sophia is *not* a separate female "Goddess" who is eternally co-existent with a male God. Besides being unfounded conjecture, such a faulty concept is illogical in a couple of respects. Firstly, if "God" is defined as the "one supreme being," then logically there can't exist *two* supreme beings, a God and a Goddess. Secondly, for two deities to exist separate and apart from each other, they would logically have to exist within a greater something that would contain them both. This greater something would therefore be the supreme God.

Moreover, the erroneous notion that there exists a separate Goddess "Trinity" demonstrates a total lack of understanding regarding the Divine Trinity. In neo-pagan and wiccan belief, for example, the Triple Goddess is not a true Trinity since "Maiden (or Virgin), Mother and Crone" are not distinct divine-persons; but merely time-phases or life-stages of the Goddess.[8] Furthermore, since two separate supreme deities cannot logically exist together, postulating a female trinity existing alongside a male trinity is simply irrational supposition that doesn't correspond with spiritual reality.

Clearly a great many modern-day religious theorists have gone to great speculative lengths to introduce a feminine complement to God, instead of concluding the obvious—the Holy Spirit is the feminine personification of divine-wisdom; and as such, is familiarly designated the Holy Mother and the Divine Sophia. Moreover, with the true Divine Trinity of Father, Mother and Son (Child), there is no need to hypothetically formulate a Goddess or a feminine Trinity in a desperately-gratuitous intellectual attempt to provide divine gender balance.

4.3 The Holy Mother as the "Substance" of the Divine Nature

The omnipotent will of the Heavenly Father can be understood as the "divine-force" *which causes movement* within the transcendent nature of God; and the omniscient wisdom of the Holy Mother can likewise be understood as the "divine-substance" within the transcendent nature of God *that is moved*.

The esoteric notion that the Holy Mother is the Trinitarian personification of divine substance is wonderfully enhanced by the etymology of the word, "substance." Substance is derived from the Latin "sub" = under, and "stāns" = to stand. Literally, then, "substance" means "to understand." Etymologically, then, divine understanding is the substance of God; and since the Holy Mother is the Trinitarian personification of omniscient, all-knowing wisdom—or divine understanding—she is the substance of God's transcendent nature.

Historically, the word "spirit" has been used as a term for the substance of the divine nature. As the Trinitarian personification of divine-substance, therefore, the Holy Mother has also been more commonly known as the "Holy Spirit."

4.4 The Holy Spirit (Mother) as the Ultimate Source of All Universal Matter

Another wonderfully-profound word etymology in

connection with the Holy Mother is the Latin word for matter or substance—"māteria." Māteria is derived from "māter," the Lain word for mother. As this etymology accurately indicates, "matter is derived from mother"; or in more comprehensive esoteric terms, all matter in the universe is derived from the divine-substance of the Holy Mother.

All matter in the universe, from the coarsest to the finest, is esoterically understood to be different levels of spirit densification; that is, lower vibratory levels of the spirit-substance of the Holy Mother. Moreover, since spirit-substance is equivalent to divine-wisdom, all material substance in the universe inherently embodies divine-wisdom to a greater or lesser degree. Further elaboration of this topic will be pursued in the Chapter 5.

CHAPTER 5

UNIVERSAL WISDOM AS THE COSMIC REFLECTION OF THE DIVINE SOPHIA

5.1 The Universe as a Living, Sentient Macrocosmic Being

A GREAT DEAL of needless and exasperating confusion regarding "Who or what is Sophia?" has been due to numerous esoteric theorists not recognizing or acknowledging the clearly-observable spiritual fact that wisdom pervades the entire universe; and manifests in a multiplicity of substances, shapes, life-forms and beings—from lowly expression to exalted degree.

Moreover, even though universal wisdom (in its wide variety of forms) is always a *feminine* expression, it is not necessarily *personified* in a confusing array of independent "Sophia-beings." In order to understand why this is so, it is necessary to esoterically understand how the cosmos was divinely created; and more specifically, how is the Divine Sophia (Holy Mother) reflected within the universe.

To begin with, except for the veiled Rosicrucian

Fraternity, few Western esotericists today fully understand or knowingly comprehend that the entire universe is a single, vast and majestic universal-being who is macrocosmically alive and elevatedly self-aware. Throughout history, this universal-being has been known by a variety of names: in Platonic philosophy as the "World Soul" (or "Anima Mundi" in Latin); in the Jewish mystical Kabbalah as the "original man" or "Adam Kadmon"; in Gnosticism as the "Primal Beginning" or "Anthropos"; and in Hindu philosophy as "Purusha" or the "Cosmic Man." In esoteric-Christianity, the universal-being is known as the "Logos-Word."

5.2 The Logos-Word as the Divine Self-Concept

The universal-being, or Logos-Word, is not eternally and infinitely self-existent (like God); but is instead a temporal and finite creation of God. Transcendently analogous to a human individual psychologically formulating a self-concept of who they are, the Logos-Word is God's self-concept of who he is. A self-concept—whether human or divine—is of course not an actual duplication of the real person; but simply a mental reflection or image of that person.

Even though God cannot logically create a second, eternally-existent, uncreated God, he can create (and has created) a perfect image or reflection of himself in the form of a divine self-concept—the Logos-Word. But unlike the transitory and evanescent self-concepts of human individuals, the divine self-concept of the Logos-Word is consciously alive and imbued with an independent will. Transcendently analogous to the human word-symbol (or logo) of self-existence—"I am"—the universal being is the "Great I AM," the Logos-Word of God (please refer to Figure 3 on the following page for a diagrammatical representation).

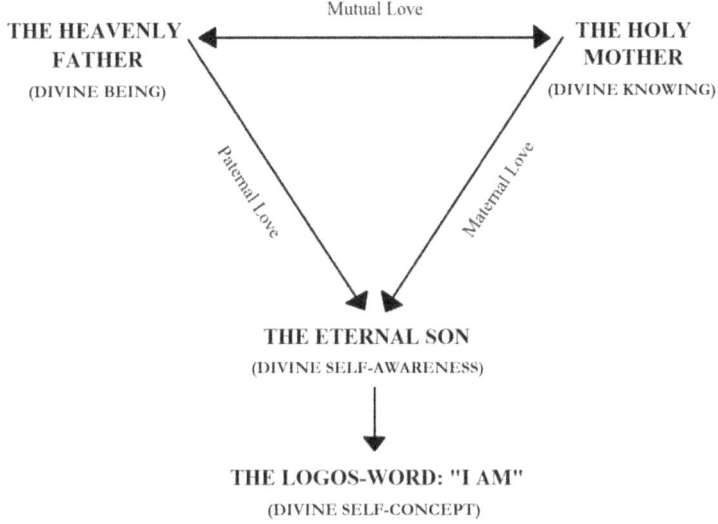

Figure 3: The Creation of the Logos-Word as Divine Self-Concept

5.3 The Divine Self-Concept of the Logos-Word and the Divine Self-Consciousness of the Eternal Son

As with human psychology, it's important to understand that divine self-awareness is fundamentally different than the divine self-concept. To be sure, there is a profoundly-intimate connection between the two—obviously there can be no self-concept without the prior existence of self-awareness. Nevertheless, as previously discussed in Chapter 2, self-conscious awareness is a permanent and essential requirement of personhood; whereas a self-concept, though beneficial, is simply a transitory mental creation.

Understood in relation to God, supernal self-awareness is an eternal and infinite *divine-person*—the Eternal Son; whereas the supernal self-concept is a temporal and finite *universal-person*—the Logos-Word. The Eternal Son is an uncreated

"God-Person"; whereas the Logos-Word is a divinely-created "God-like person."

Not surprisingly, then, the direct connection and consequent dependence of the divine self-concept with divine self-awareness has resulted in Western theology mistakenly equating the two; that is, the Trinitarian Son is theologically considered to be one and the same as the Logos-Word.[9]

5.4 The Trinitarian Reflection of the Logos-Word

Since the divine self-concept was created "in the image and likeness" of God, the macrocosmic nature of the Logos-Word faithfully reflects and mirrors the three divine-persons of the Trinity: the Heavenly Father, the Holy Mother and the Eternal Son. The universal-person of the Logos-Word, therefore, is also fundamentally threefold in nature. But this is not a unity of three divine-persons (as with God); but rather, a unity of three "universal principles." The Heavenly Father is reflected in the Logos-Word as the "universal masculine-principle"; the Holy Mother is reflected in the Logos-Word as the "universal feminine-principle"; and the Eternal Son is reflected in the Logos-Word as the "principle of universal harmony."

Since the Heavenly Father divinely personifies the force of omnipotent will, the universal masculine-principle of the Logos-Word can also be referred to as the "principle of universal will." Likewise, since the Holy Mother divinely personifies the substance of omniscient wisdom, the universal feminine principle of the Logos-Word can also be referred to as the "principle of universal wisdom." Furthermore, since the Eternal Son divinely personifies the unity of parental love, the Logos-Word's fundamental principle of universal harmony can also be referred to as the "principle of universal love" (please refer to Figure 4 on the following page).

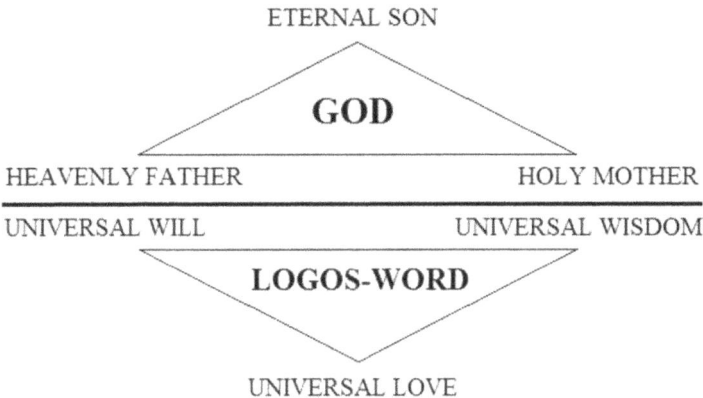

Figure 4: The Threefold Nature of the Logos-Word

5.5 Universal Wisdom (Sophia) as an Essential Attribute of the Logos-Word

From the foregoing esoteric information, it is clearly evident that the wisdom which pervades the entire universe is a reflection of the Holy Mother—the Divine Sophia. As such, universal wisdom is feminine in nature, but it is not separately personified. Universal wisdom is the feminine, maternal aspect of the Logos-Word.

As a lower vibration of the Holy Spirit-Mother, universal wisdom provides the underlying substance for all the materializations of form that occur throughout the universe. Moreover, the feminine-principle of universal wisdom manifests as the expanding, propagating and proliferating activity on all levels of universal existence. All life-forms, from subatomic particles to celestial seraphim, incorporate and utilize the universal feminine-principle of wisdom to various degrees.

UNIVERSAL WISDOM AS THE REFLECTION OF THE DIVINE SOPHIA

Universal wisdom (sophia) can also be correctly regarded as the mental substance, the mind, of the Logos-Word. Therefore, universal wisdom-sophia, though feminine in nature, is not a separate being; but rather, belongs to the universal-person of the Logos-Word. Many examples in the confusing array of Sophia titles—such as the heavenly-sophia, the earthly-sophia, the goddess Sophia, the Aeon Sophia, the Virgin Sophia, Sophia-Achamoth, Pistis Sophia, Isis-Sophia, Jesus Sophia, theo-sophia, philo-sophia and anthropo-sophia—are *not* separate beings; but are instead various manifestations of the universal wisdom-sophia that belongs to the Logos-Word. Some of these various manifestations will be discussed in greater detail in the following chapter.

CHAPTER 6:

HISTORICAL MANIFESTATIONS OF UNIVERSAL WISDOM-SOPHIA

6.1 The Background Mythology of the Egyptian Goddess, Isis

TO SUMMARIZE AND emphasize what has been esoterically asserted thus far, there is only one supernal feminine-being in existence who perfectly personifies divine wisdom itself, and that is the Holy Spirit—one of the three divine-persons of the Blessed Trinity. In esoteric-Christianity, the Holy Spirit is better known and recognized as the Holy Mother, the divine personification of the eternal-feminine nature of God. It is she, and she alone, who is truthfully acknowledged to be the "Divine (or Holy) Sophia."

As a divine-person of the Trinity, then, there can be no creation of a second Divine Sophia, a second deific personification of God's feminine wisdom-nature. Therefore, throughout the entire created cosmos, though there are numerous advanced beings who embody and manifest divine wisdom to various degrees, there are none who are equal to—or who can properly be called—the Divine Sophia.

The highest reflection of the Divine Sophia within the created universe (the Logos-Word) is a feminine-*principle* of wisdom, not a feminine-*person* of wisdom. Moreover, this feminine-principle of wisdom—or "cosmic intelligence"—is a fundamental attribute belonging to only one universal-person—the Logos-Word.

Certainly, as a feminine-principle, universal wisdom (or cosmic intelligence) can be grammatically referred to as "she" and "her." But since cosmic wisdom-intelligence is not an individuated-being or actualized-person, when the word "sophia" is used in connection with this universal feminine-principle, it should not be capitalized in order to avoid misunderstanding and confusion. The fact that numerous esoteric theorists have carelessly capitalized the various historical manifestations of universal wisdom-sophia, has for decades frustrated and obscured a clear understanding of the Divine Sophia and her integral activity throughout cosmic creation.

Take, for example, the historical manifestation of "Isis-Sophia" as originally encountered in ancient Egyptian mythology, and as later obscured by today's esoteric theorists. Most likely, the mythological figure of Isis began as an actual historical queen who, together with her husband Osirus, ruled Egypt sometime during the Old Kingdom, around 3000 BC.

According to Greek historian Plutarch (c.AD 46–AD 120), Osirus was drowned by his brother, Set, who later scattered his dismembered body throughout Egypt so that it wouldn't be found by Isis. Isis, however, did manage to recollect most of the strewn body parts; and thereby resurrect the dead Osirus in the underworld. Shortly afterwards, through a magical process, Isis was able to give birth to a son, named Horus.

Over time, the details of the Isis myth gradually assumed archetypal significance, and Isis herself gradually acquired deific stature. By the fifth century BC, during Graeco-Roman times, Isis had become a popularly-worshipped goddess—referred to as the "Queen of Heaven"—and often equated with Demeter and Athena. By the first and second centuries AD, Isis had elevatedly become the divine embodiment of wisdom, and the universal mother who "veiled" and guarded the secret truths of nature.

According to Plutarch, Isis was "a goddess exceptionally wise and a lover of wisdom, to whom, as her name at least seems to indicate, knowledge and understanding are in the highest degree appropriate" (*Isis and Osiris*; 1st century AD). Furthermore, in a novel by Roman writer Apuleius (c.124–c.170 AD), Isis herself declares: "I am nature, the universal Mother, mistress of all the elements, primordial child of time, sovereign of all things spiritual (*The Golden Ass*; 2nd century AD).

6.2 Interpreting the Mythological Symbolism of Isis-Sophia

In the eyes of esoteric-Christianity, there is no goddess-being named Isis or Isis-Sophia. While in ancient times there may have existed an actual Egyptian queen from which the Isis-myth arose, over time any historical persons or events became representative symbols that conveyed a more universal and cosmic meaning.

The myth of Isis is best understood as an allegorical description, in mythological form, of the profound psychological developments that were occurring within the collective soul of humanity during the Egyptian and the Graeco-Roman cultural eras. During that time, mankind was gradually acquiring the cognitive capacity of abstract, intellectual thought, and concomitantly unfolding increased ego-awareness. Unfortunately, however, these progressive developments resulted in the loss of mankind's innate spiritual oneness with the natural world.

As pictorially conveyed in the Isis myth, the goddess Isis symbolically represents the feminine-principle of universal wisdom (cosmic intelligence). Her royal consort, the god Osirus, symbolically represents the masculine-principle of universal being. According to the mythological story, Osirus is drowned by his jealous brother, Set; who later dismembers his body and then buries the parts throughout Egypt.

Esoterically interpreted, Set symbolically represents Ahriman, the adversarial spirit of material darkness.[10] During the Egyptian and Graeco-Roman cultural eras, the materialistic influencing of Ahriman (Set) increasingly directed human sense perception away from the spiritual world; and instead, directed it to the physical world of outer nature. As a result, mankind's innate oneness with universal being (Osirus) was gradually extinguished (drowned), and fragmentally concealed (dismembered and buried) within the sensory physical world (Egypt).

During this transitional period of human development, the activity of universal wisdom (Isis) was still able to overcome the perceptual fragmentation of universal being (Osirus), and retain the primordial sense of universal oneness within the collective subconsciousness of mankind (resurrect Osirus within the underworld). Fortunately as well, the Ahrimanic fracturing of universal oneness actually enabled and stimulated the development of individual ego-awareness (the birth of Horus) from out of the maternal forces of universal wisdom (Isis) acting within the human soul.

6.3 The Pre-Christian Symbolism of Mother Isis and the Child Horus

From the preceding symbolism, the image of Isis with her

child Horus—that was often depicted in ancient sculpture and painting (such as Figure 5 below)—is esoterically understood to convey profound cosmic meaning.

Figure 5: Mother Isis and the Child Horus

During the ancient Egyptian and Graeco-Roman cultural eras, the archetypal image of mother and child—that was artistically represented as Isis and Horus—symbolized the birth of individual ego-consciousness that began during those eras. The goddess Isis represented the substance of cosmic wisdom that was incorporated within humanity as the sentient, intellectual and consciousness soul vehicles. It is the indwelling integration and embodiment of these three soul vehicles that unfolds and develops individual self-consciousness (ego-awareness). The "I-consciousness" that was developed in mankind during that time was symbolically represented as the "Eye of Horus" (see Figure 6 below).

Figure 6: The Eye ("I") of Horus

6.4 Esoterically Understanding Philo-Sophia

As with Isis-Sophia, esoteric-Christianity does not recognize a goddess or hierarchical-being called "Philo-Sophia" either. Once again, the feminine-figure of Philo-Sophia (Philosophy) is understood to symbolically represent a significant cognitive stage in human evolution that began in Graeco-Roman times (Figure 7 below is a depiction of "Lady" Philosophy taken from a painting by Raphael around 1509).

Figure 7: Philo-Sophia (Philosophy) from Raphael

Prior to acquiring the cognitive capacity of intellectual thinking; that is, the mental ability to freely generate and manipulate abstract thoughts within the mind, mankind had a passive relationship to cosmic intelligence (universal wisdom). Knowledge was acquired by the passive reception of thoughts and ideas that were generated in the human mind by external supernatural forces and beings. To ancient Greek experience, these supernatural sources of cognition were imaginatively seen as gods, muses, daimons or fates.

In the distant, pre-intellectual past, then, humanity experienced an innate spiritual oneness with nature, and cosmic wisdom flowed into the mind in a dreamily-clairvoyant, instinctual way. With the development of intellectual thought, Classical Greek thinkers—for the first time in human history—could be actively engaged in the pursuit of universal knowledge. They could cognitively reach out into the surrounding cosmos and consciously seek out the underlying wisdom-sophia of nature. To the ancient Egyptian, on the other hand, the truths of nature (Isis) were mysterious and fearful secrets that were hidden behind a veil of obscurity that no mortal could lift.[11]

Not surprisingly, ancient Greek thinkers were totally enamoured and thoroughly infatuated with the newly-acquired capacity for intellectual thought. They were, indeed, lovers ("philos") of this now-approachable wisdom of nature ("sophia") and the fact that human minds could begin to gradually lift the veil of nature's secret knowledge.

Through residual clairvoyant perception, the ancient Greek thinker understood that cosmic wisdom-knowledge (sophia) was feminine in nature; and was therefore an important attribute of several goddesses, such as Athena, Selene, Artemis, Gaia and Astraea. In the ancient Greek pantheon, however, there was no direct personification of universal truth—there was no goddess of wisdom named "Sophia."

6.5 "Lady Philosophy" in the Sixth-Century Literature of Boethius

The intellectual pursuit of knowledge that eventually became known as "philosophy" was also personified by some famous writers during the Medieval period of European history. One noteworthy writer, for example, the Roman senator and philosopher Boethius (c.480–524 AD), while unjustly imprisoned and awaiting execution, wrote a highly-influential treatise entitled *The Consolation of Philosophy* (523 AD). During his confinement, Boethius had the opportunity to solitarily reflect on a range of profound philosophical issues; such as God and evil, fate and happiness, fame and wealth, and free-will and determinism.

In order to effectively convey his deep philosophical insights in written form, Boethius placed them in the context of a Socratic dialogue between himself and "Lady Philosophy." Clearly with Boethius, the feminization and personification of philosophical wisdom was a very clever literary device, and not a literal assertion that there existed an actual being called Lady Philosophy. Moreover, as a Platonic thinker living in the sixth century who was warmly disposed to monotheistic Christianity, it is quite unlikely that Boethius believed in the existence of an obscure deity or some Roman goddess named Lady Philosophy.

6.6 "Lady Philosophy" in the Thirteenth-Century Love Poetry of Dante

Boethius, through *The Consolation of Philosophy*, had an enormous influence on European Christian thinkers throughout the Middle Ages. One such thinker was the famous Italian poet, Dante Alighieri (c.1265–1321). As a young man, Dante was totally infatuated with a young Florentine woman named Beatrice Portinari (1266–1290) who he had originally met when she was eight, and he was nine years old.

Later in life, since he was formally married to another, Dante could only platonically love Beatrice from afar. Moreover, in true courtly love ("fin'amor") tradition, in Dante's early poetry, he idolized and idealized his unrequited lover as a paragon of sublime beauty and virtue.

Not surprisingly, then, when Beatrice tragically died at the tender age of twenty-four, Dante was psychologically devastated. For several years after Beatrice's death, Dante submerged his sorrow and loss in the fervent study of Latin; the philosophy of Boethius, Cicero and St. Thomas Aquinas; Dominican and Franciscan theology; and Italian poetry.

Boethius and *The Consolation of Philosophy* made an enormous impact on Dante during his period of mourning. Moreover, when writing *Il Convivio* ("The Banquet"; c.1304–1307) Dante also employed Boethius' "Lady Philosophy" as his own poetic personification. In his own words:

> By "my lady" I mean the same lady whose meaning I addressed in the previous canzone, namely that most virtuous light, Philosophy, whose rays make flowers bloom and bear the fruit of mankind's true nobility. (Commentary on Book Four)

Unlike the allegorical figure of Beatrice in Dante's poetry—who was based on a real-life person—there's no compelling reason to believe that Dante considered the allegorical Lady Philosophy in his poetry to be an actual living being.

Noteworthy as well, the role and influence of Dante's Lady Philosophy differs somewhat from Boethius' Lady Philosophy. In Boethius' case, human intellectual thinking—personified as Lady Philosophy—provides him with consolation and understanding regarding the injustice and misfortune of his imprisonment. In Dante's case, his quest is the search for true love; and while the "love of wisdom"—Lady Philosophy—is considered to be superior to carnal love, Dante does not regard her as the highest form of love.

In his later, more famous work, *La Divina Commedia* ("The Divine Comedy"; c.1308–1320), the love of human knowledge (Lady Philosophy) is superseded by the love of divine wisdom (theology), allegorically personified as "my Lady" Beatrice. As Dante's poetic spirit-guide, Beatrice leads Dante to a vision of the Divine Trinity, and the comprehension that God is the source and object of true love: "the Love that moves the Sun and the other stars" (*Paradiso Canto XXXIII*).

Even though Lady Philosophy is only a literary device and not an actual living being to both Dante and Boethius, it is nevertheless noteworthy that for both Medieval writers, the "love of wisdom"—philosophy—was as intense and tangible as the love between flesh-and-blood men and women. Sadly, this is certainly not the case today.

Furthermore, it is once again important to keep in mind that even though universal wisdom-sophia (as the underlying intelligence of the cosmos) is *not* an independent, celestial goddess-being, it *is* feminine substance that is suffused with supernal life and consciousness, and which truly belongs to an actual universal being—the Logos-Word. Universal wisdom-sophia is the underlying mental substance of the cosmos—"the life-filled, superconscious mind of nature"—rightfully regarded as the "feminine side" of the Logos-Word.

CHAPTER 7:

THE LUCIFERIC DISTORTION OF WISDOM-SOPHIA: THE NEW ISIS-MYTH

7.1 The Unreliability of Human Intellection

AS DANTE INDICATED in his epic poem, *The Divine Comedy*, human intellection—such as philosophy—does not necessarily lead to the highest truth; but instead, can be a rather unreliable distraction. As every intellectual thinker knows from personal experience, the cognitive capacity to generate one's own thoughts is no guarantee that those thoughts will conform to reality, to actually correspond to objective truth.

The unfortunate fact that human intellection is continually prone to error and falsehood necessitated the scientific method for determining validity in the study of nature. In this case, it is a scientific requirement that any newly-generated intellectual idea (a "hypothesis") must be empirically tested in order to reliably determine the truth or falseness of the idea.

Fortunately, the current unreliability of intellectual thinking to accurately ascertain the underlying truths of nature (universal wisdom-sophia) is only a temporary stage in human cognitive development. According to spiritual-scientific research, when human beings first came into existence during Lemurian times,[12] the internal soul forces were not yet sufficiently developed to generate intellectual thought. Instead, truthful knowledge and information was originally acquired in the form of internal astral imaginations, rather than clear intellectual concepts. During those distant prehistoric times, vivid picture-images that directly corresponded to the surrounding environment spontaneously arose in the human astral body through the external agency of superphysical forces and beings.

In the primal beginning, then, the human astral body faithfully mirrored external cosmic truth—universal wisdom-sophia. Unfortunately for nascent humanity, this instinctual picture-consciousness of cosmic wisdom did not continue for very long. As allegorically conveyed in the biblical book of Genesis—there was a devious snake in paradise that changed the destined course of human events.

7.2 The Beginning of Luciferic Interference in Human Evolution

Soon after our Lemurian ancestors acquired rudimentary self-consciousness and free-will, their emergent astral bodies were subtly penetrated by a powerful, supernatural adversarial-being known as Lucifer (Latin for "Light-bearer"). Like Ahriman, Lucifer has been actively opposed to the progressive evolution of humanity and the earth since prehistoric times. By injecting false and distorted picture-images into human astral consciousness, Lucifer intentionally distorted cosmic truth; thereby causing a serious rupture in humanity's connection with its divinely-appointed overseers. This disastrous historical occurrence has been allegorically described in the Bible as the "expulsion from the Garden of Eden."

In consequence of Luciferic interference, primeval human beings were seduced into generating their own false astral images, which in turn enticed them into behaving contrary to the divine will as reflected in creation. In other words, through Luciferic corruption of cosmic wisdom-sophia in human astral bodies, nascent mankind slowly descended into falsehood, error, dishonesty and evil.

7.3 The Luciferic Corruption of Intellectual Truth

During the Graeco-Roman cultural era (which began in 747 BC), mankind began to internally unfold and develop the intellectual soul vehicle, and its capacity to generate intellectual thought. Unfortunately, the acquisition of intellectual thinking necessitated a corresponding loss of clairvoyant picture-consciousness. As a result, the instinctual experience of passively receiving cosmic wisdom-truth from external supernatural sources in the form of dream-like astral images gradually disappeared from human consciousness.

In its place, human beings were able to actively seek out cosmic wisdom-truth; and to convey this self-acquired knowledge in the form of clear intellectual concepts, rather than in nebulous picture-images. Unfortunately, the intellectual avenue to cosmic truth, the cognitive access to wisdom-sophia, was veiled by Luciferic distortion and interference.

As an adversarial-being, Lucifer characteristically exaggerates, overextends, super-expands and hyper-inflates cosmic wisdom-truth in his own consciousness. He does this by taking the universal feminine-force of centrifugal expansion, propagation and embellishment to an extreme outward degree. By doing so, he distorts, degrades and destroys cosmic wisdom-sophia within himself. Unfortunately, by covertly insinuating himself into the intellectual souls of unsuspecting humanity, Lucifer has also confounded the access to cosmic truth for human intellectual thinking. The Luciferic forces of hyper-inflation within the human intellectual soul produces intellectual thoughts known as "abstractions." In this case, abstractions are intellectual thoughts that are separated and estranged from true reality.

Rather than leading human thought to cosmic truths that are full of life, consciousness, morality and meaning, abstract intellection conveys a universe that is lifeless, insensate, amoral and purposeless. Such is the worldview of materialistic science that is based on Luciferically-induced, abstract intellection.

7.4 A Modern-Day Isis-Myth of Human Cognition

The present-day phase of human cognitive development can be pictorially conveyed and esoterically understood in the form of a revised Isis-myth. In the Egyptian version of the Isis-myth, mankind's innate oneness with universal-being (Osiris) was shattered, compressed and interred throughout the material world by Ahriman (Set). In the modern-day version of the Isis-myth, universal wisdom-truth (Isis-Sophia) is unlawfully seized by Lucifer (Typhon),[13] diffused throughout the farthest regions of space, and abstracted into lifeless universal laws and mechanical celestial motions.

In the Egyptian myth, universal wisdom-truth (Isis) was able to salvage and retain universal oneness of being (Osiris) within the subconscious mind of mankind (the underworld); and thereby give birth to increased ego-awareness (Horus). In the modern-day myth, Christ-infused self-awareness (the transformed Horus) has the power to extend into the bright outer cosmos and revive the life-filled, universal wisdom-truth (Isis); as well as to penetrate into the dark material world (the underworld) and raise up universal oneness of being (Osirus) into day-consciousness once again.

In a lecture given on 24 December 1920 entitled "Search for the New Isis, the Divine Sophia: The Quest for the Isis-Sophia," Rudolf Steiner succinctly conveyed this modern-day Isis-myth in the form of an evocative poem:

> Isis- Sophia,
> Wisdom of God;
> Lucifer has slain her,
> And on wings of cosmic forces
> Carried her away into the depths of space.
> Christ-will,
> Working in us;
> Shall tear her from Lucifer;
> And on grounds of spiritual knowledge
> Call to new life in human souls,
> Isis- Sophia,
> Wisdom of God.

7.5 Christ-Jesus and the Divine Rescue of Cosmic Truth (Isis-Sophia)

As powerful superplanetary-beings, Lucifer and Ahriman far outmatched nascent mankind. It took an equally-powerful celestial-being—the Solar-Christos, regent of our sun—to overcome these adversarial-beings, undo their extensive damage and restore human access to pristine, undistorted cosmic truth. By indwelling the man Jesus, and uniting himself with the divine Son through the Logos-Word, the Solar-Christos (or "Christ") was able to infuse the human soul with the power of divine love. Through the power of divine love, Christ-Jesus was able to access and incarnate celestial and godly truth to such a degree, that in a real sense he personified this truth and could rightfully declare: "I am the way, and the truth, and the life" (John 14:6).

Expressed in more mythological terms, only the power of divine love (the Christed-Horus) was able to wrest universal wisdom-truth (Isis-Sophia) from the cognitive clutches of Lucifer (Typhon); and wrest universal oneness of being (Osirus) from the perceptual grasp of Ahriman (Set).

So, for individual human beings in the Christian era to effectively pierce the veil of abstract Luciferic thinking in order to access the living truth of the macrocosmic Logos-Word, it is absolutely necessary to unite oneself with Christ-Jesus.[14] This was superlatively demonstrated by the Christ-imbued authors of New Testament, such as St. Matthew, St. Mark, St. Luke, St. John and St. Paul. The intellectual truth conveyed in their writings is free from Luciferic distortion and falsehood.

Christ-enabled intellectual freedom from Luciferic falsehood was also demonstrated by the profound theology of the Early Church Fathers, especially the Eight Doctors of the Church: St. Ambrose (340–397), St. Jerome (347–420), St. Augustine (354–430), St. Gregory the Great (540–604), St. Basil (c.329–379), St. Athanasius (c.296–373), St. Gregory of Nazianzus (329–c.389) and St. John Chrysostom (347–407).

Truth-filled intellectual thinking continued throughout the Middle Ages with Christian theologians and philosophers, such as John Scotus Eriugena (c.815–c.877) and St. Anselm of Canterbury (1033–1109).[15] Christianized intellectual thinking during this time reached its pinnacle of achievement with the eminent Scholastic theologian and philosopher, St. Thomas Aquinas (1225–1274).

Unfortunately, with the start of the Renaissance and continuing into the Modern era, intellectual access to the spiritual world and to universal wisdom-truth became increasingly darkened by the rapid spread of "materialism": the belief that nothing exists except matter; and that only what can be measured and perceived with the five physical senses is real. Therefore, according to materialism, the spiritual world does not exist (The rise of materialism will be discussed in more detail in Chapter 8).

7.6 Gnosticism as a Luciferic Distortion of Cosmic Truth

In the centuries immediately before and after the incarnation of Christ-Jesus, there existed a diverse collection of pagan religious sects that shared a common, eclectic ideology later known as "Gnosticism."[16] Originally, Gnosticism combined elements of Persian Zoroastrianism, Graeco-Roman mystery religion, Platonic philosophy, Hellenistic Judaism, Babylonian astrology and Egyptian Hermeticism into a uniquely-phantasmagoric worldview. Not surprisingly, then, with the rise of Christianity, Gnosticism also eagerly added a mélange of mangled Christian concepts into its ideological stew.

Even though ancient Gnosticism loosely incorporated Christian personalities, events and terminology, it radically deviated from the spiritual truths that were conveyed by Christ-Jesus through the apostles, the early disciples and the Church Fathers. Not surprisingly then, pseudo-Christian Gnosticism was declared heretical by the early Church.

Gnostic cosmology, as exemplified in the *Pistis Sophia*, is a perfect example of Luciferically-distorted cosmic truth. To esoteric perception, it is clear that gnostic writers retained access to the highest levels of spiritual existence; but without being adequately imbued with the true Christ-spirit, their spiritual perception and comprehension was distorted, exaggerated, falsified, and metamorphosized by Luciferic interference.

The dizzying and confusing cacophony of exotic celestial

beings contained in the *Pistis Sophia*—aeons, paralemptores, light maidens, sphaira, archontes, probolai, topoi, apatores, tripneumatoi, hymneutai, amenytoi, asemantoi, anennoetoi, asaleutoi, akinetoi, realms of the midst, realms of the right and left, and light treasures—bears no resemblance to the celestial hierarchy as understood in Western theology—angels, archangels, principalities, powers and so on.

It is clear from reading the gnostic writings that were discovered near Nag Hammadi in 1945, that the figures of Jesus and his disciples were nothing more than literary devices to convey previously-established gnostic ideology. In other words, they were entirely fictitious accounts of the life and teachings of Christ-Jesus. Moreover, the notion (championed by some modern-day, roseate adherents) that Gnosticism better celebrates the "feminine in all things"—than does conventional Christianity—is soundly contradicted in the gnostic Gospel of Thomas which states:

> Simon Peter said to them: "Let Mary [Magdalene] go forth from among us, for women are not worthy of the life." Jesus said: "Behold, I shall lead her, that I may make her male, in order that she also may become a living spirit like you males. For every woman who makes herself male shall enter into the kingdom of heaven."(Thomas: 114)

CHAPTER 8:

AHRIMANIC MATERIALISM AND THE BIRTH OF ANTHROPO-SOPHIA

8.1 The Rapid Rise of Ahrimanic Materialism in the Modern Age

EVEN THOUGH CHRIST-JESUS had overcome the falsifying, truth-distorting influences of Lucifer and Ahriman in his own life on earth, these adversarial beings still retained a stranglehold on most other human intellection that has continued into the Modern era. While Lucifer has been the primary adversarial being throughout humanity's prehistoric past, since the beginning of the Modern era (around 1500), Ahriman has rapidly increased his corrupting influence on intellectual thought.

Whereas Lucifer corrupts the universal feminine-principle of centrifugal expansion by outwardly distending to an extreme degree, Ahriman corrupts the universal masculine-principle of centripetal contraction by inwardly compressing to an extreme degree. A defining characteristic of Ahriman, therefore, is his incessant compulsion to squeeze and compress all spiritual substance into dense matter. In other words, Ahriman seeks to obliterate all knowledge of the spiritual realm and live only in the material world.

Consequently, Ahrimanic influencing within the human soul throughout the Modern era has forcefully directed attention away from the spiritual realm, and focused it exclusively on the material world—the world of matter and energy perceptible to the five physical senses. As a result, human intellectual thinking has become increasingly more materialistic, physicalistic, secular and atheistic.

Up until the mid-nineteenth century, access to cosmic truth—universal wisdom-sophia—became increasingly more difficult, and darkened to human intellectual perception. As Ahriman had concealed ("buried") universal oneness of being in the "grave of matter" during the ancient Egyptian age, he now strives to entomb cosmic spiritual-truth in the sepulcher of matter during the current Modern age.

8.2   Nineteenth-Century Materialism and the Ahrimanic War in Heaven

The rapid rise of Ahrimanic materialism resulted in a serious spiritual crisis by the mid-nineteenth century. An increased number of souls that had been spiritually darkened by Ahrimanic materialism carried that darkness with them after death. The collective darkness began to seriously shadow and suffocate the superphysical region closest to the earth—the etheric realm.

Ahriman and his supernatural subordinates saw this dire situation as an evil opportunity to condense and materialize the entire etheric sphere of the earth. As well, this Ahrimanic horde mounted an attack on the etheric life-body of Christ-Jesus in the realm of Shambhala. Since the evil adversarial powers had failed to destroy the physical body of Christ-Jesus through crucifixion, they sought to destroy his etheric body instead through etheric paralysis and densification.

Though the Ahrimanic assassins managed to briefly eclipse the spiritual consciousness of Christ-Jesus—a condition resembling physical death—they were beaten back and defeated in 1879 by the celestial legions of holiness, led by the great servant of the Lord, Archangel Michael.[17] Moreover, analogous to his physical resurrection, through the power of divine love Christ-Jesus also restored his Ahrimanically-assaulted etheric body to even greater glory than before.

Following St. Michael's victory in this modern-day "war in heaven," the defeated Ahrimanic assailants were cast out of "heaven" (the upper-atmospheric etheric realm), and exiled to the "earth" (the lower-subterranean etheric realm). As a triumphant result, unfettered access to universal wisdom-truth (Isis-Sophia) through human intellect was made available for the first time in cosmic history.

Furthermore, by dispelling the dark miasmatic veil of Ahrimanic materialism in the etheric sphere, the pathway was cleared for Christ-Jesus to begin appearing on earth in his resurrected etheric body.[18] This earthly appearance of Christ-Jesus in etheric form that began in the early-twentieth century is what esoteric-Christianity understands as the "second coming of Christ."

8.3 St. Michael's Descent to the Earth and the Formation of Spiritual Science

Fortunately, when the Ahrimanic insurgents were cast out of heaven and exiled to earth in 1879, unsuspecting humanity was not left defenseless. In order to protect unwary human beings from these new evil inhabitants, the great Archangel Michael superphysically descended to earth as well.

Moreover, after assisting Christ-Jesus in clearing an intellectual pathway to universal cosmic-truth, St. Michael has tirelessly laboured since then to guard this pathway for mankind. Consequently, St. Michael is esoterically known as the "protector of cosmic intelligence."

Furthermore, in order to provide a reliable and effective methodology to intellectually acquire, compile and systematize universal wisdom-truth from a human perspective, St. Michael established the first authentic "science of the spirit" through the inspired activity of Christian-esotericist and philosopher, Rudolf Steiner (1861–1925).[19] Instead of passively receiving spiritual truth in the form of dream-like revelations (as occurred throughout prehistoric times), human beings could now investigate, study and verify spiritual truth for themselves in a scientific-intellectual way.

8.4 The Birth of Anthropo-Sophia: The "Wisdom of Mankind"

Since the science of the spirit actively studies and acquires cosmic wisdom-truth from a human perspective—rather than passively receiving it from a celestial, hierarchical perspective—it is an "anthropo-centric" spiritual science. As such, the spiritual wisdom-truth (sophia) that is acquired by human beings (anthropos) has been termed, "anthroposophy."

Anthroposophy can also be understood, then, as the *once-external* cosmic wisdom that can now be incorporated *within the internal* constitution of mankind. Since all humanly-internalized wisdom-truth (anthropo-sophia) also contributes to the collective wisdom of the universe (the Logos-Word), anthropo-sophia also increasingly becomes an integral aspect of external cosmic truth. This does not mean that anthropo-sophia has become an individualized goddess-being; but simply become a part of the universal mind, the feminine nature of the Logos-Word.

The internal to external objectification of anthropo-centric wisdom-truth—anthroposophy—was explained by Rudolf Steiner in a lecture given on 03 February 1913 entitled "The Being Anthroposophia":

> After Sophia has entered human beings, she must take their being with her and present it to them outwardly, objectively.
>
> Sophia will become objective again, but she will take with her what humanity is, and objectively present herself in this form. Thus she will present herself not only as Sophia, but as *Anthroposophia*—as the Sophia who, after passing through the human soul, through the very being of the human being, henceforth bears that being within her. And in this form she will confront enlightened human beings as the objective being Sophia who once stood before the Greeks.

8.5 Correctly Understanding the "Being" of Anthropo-Sophia

Unfortunately, a great deal of confusion, misunderstanding and falsehood has occurred amongst anthroposophists and other esotericists by not fully understanding what Rudolf Steiner meant by the "being" of anthropo-sophia. Many have erroneously concluded that she is an actual celestial spirit or goddess-like entity.

Obviously, anthropo-sophia is not a "being" in the same sense as a "human being"; that is, she's not an individualized life-form who possesses a complex assemblage of body, soul and spiritual vehicles of expression and consciousness. Nor does she have a long history of cosmic evolution, together with other companion "beings." If anthropo-sophia did possess vehicles of expression and an evolutionary history, then she could be specifically placed within the celestial hierarchy as an angel, or a dominion, or a cherubim, for instance. But since she can't, anthropo-sophia is a "being" in a different sense.

At the very beginning of a series of four lectures on anthropo-sophia, Rudolf Steiner clarified exactly what he meant in this case:

> The next four lectures and, indeed, all the lectures that I shall deliver in the next few days will really deal with the "being," or **essence**, [emphasis mine] of Anthroposophy" (Ibid.)

Even though the word "essence" can specifically apply to an immaterial entity, in this case it is clearly an "underlying substance," and not a person. Therefore, according to Steiner, anthropo-sophia is a fundamental cosmic substance, and not a celestial entity.

Steiner's use of "being" as "essence" is also demonstrated by the quotation on the previous page: "After Sophia has entered human beings, she must take their **being** [emphasis mine] with her …" Obviously, Steiner is not suggesting that universal sophia-wisdom transports entire human persons out into cosmic space; but rather, the "essence" of cosmic-wisdom unites with the "essence" of human beings.

Substituting the word "understanding" for "substance" (please refer to Chapter sub-heading 4.3), we can also meaningfully define "essence" as "fundamental understanding" or "truth." By doing so, Steiner's phrase: "After Sophia has entered human beings, she must take their being with her …" can be interpreted to mean: "After cosmic truth has entered into human beings, she must take human truth with her …"

Once again, when referring to cosmic truth, it's important to esoterically recognize that we're referring to the universal mental substance—the feminine aspect of the Logos-Word—that is suffused with life and consciousness. And even though cosmic truth (wisdom-sophia) is not a separate being herself, she is united to the being (the masculine aspect) of the Logos-Word.

Even though universal wisdom-sophia (cosmic truth) is not an individualized entity who exists separate and apart from the universal-being of the Logos-Word, she nevertheless is incorporated into countless living beings—both human and celestial—throughout the vast cosmos. Some beings in particular, incorporate cosmic truth to a superlative degree. One such celestial being is, of course, the Solar-Christos, the regent of the sun. One such human being is, not surprisingly, Mary the mother of Jesus. Recognizing her exemplary incorporation of universal wisdom-sophia and her concomitant connection with the Holy Mother—the Divine Sophia—the following three chapters will be devoted to esoterically examining her life and mission.

CHAPTER 9:

THE DIFFERENT JESUS-FAMILIES IN ST. LUKE AND ST. MATTHEW

9.1 Mary, the Mother of Jesus, as an Important Figure in World History

WHILE THE PERSON of Mary, the mother of Jesus, has been highly venerated for centuries by the Catholic Church, most Protestant denominations have chosen to deliberately de-emphasize her biblical presence and intimate involvement in the life of Jesus (except perhaps in nativity scenes during the Christmas season). Shockingly, some fundamentalist Christians have even denounced "the Catholic Mary" as "the great whore."

Astoundingly contrariwise, the Islamic religion has historically regarded Mary as one of the most righteous women in history, devoting an entire chapter in the Qu'ran to her. Also amazing, and at the same time perplexing, despite an increasingly secular and atheistic world-culture, a December 2015 edition of National Geographic magazine declared: "Mary: The Most Powerful Woman in the World."

Clearly, given such fervent—albeit contradictory—regard, Mary is an important religious figure who is well-worth our deepest and profoundest consideration. Although Western theology has established many important spiritual truths concerning Mary that will of course be considered here, this particular discourse will comprehensively focus on spiritual information provided by the esoteric-Christian tradition, particularly the spiritual-scientific investigations of anthroposophy.

The supersensible clairvoyant research of anthroposophy will often discover spiritual truths that are new and unusual, as well as information that is much more detailed and complex than that contained in Western theology. Nevertheless, true knowledge that is conveyed by anthroposophical spiritual science will not contradict or deny the established truths of Western theology; but instead, will support, augment, clarify and expand these basic truths.

In order to adequately consider the person of Mary and her enormous contribution to human, world and cosmic advancement, profound esoteric wisdom will need to be taken into consideration regarding the Divine Trinity, the Logos-Word, the celestial hierarchy of beings (both good and bad), salvational history, and our saviour Christ-Jesus. Moreover, particular focus will be directed to Mary's special relationship with the Holy Spirit of God (also known as the Divine Sophia in esoteric-Christianity); and how this relationship is important to all mankind. From this expansive treasure of esoteric wisdom, it will become abundantly clear that Mary is truly a transformative fountain of God's grace; and not only "blessed amongst women," but supremely "blessed amongst angels and saints" as well.

9.2 Reading the Akashic Records to Clairvoyantly Study and Understand the Past

According to centuries-old esoteric knowledge, the entire universe is pervaded by an invisible superphysical substance termed "akasha." Akasha is characteristically super-sensitive to all vibratory impressions of matter, energy and mind; acting, as such, like a vast cosmic recording medium. In other words, akasha faithfully preserves and stores *every* universal event (including thoughts and feelings) for vast aeons of time. In a very real sense, then, the "akashic records" can be regarded as the "memories of nature." As additionally described in *The Aquarian Gospel of Jesus the Christ*:

> This Akashic, or primary substance, is of exquisite fineness and is so sensitive that the slightest vibrations of an ether any place in the universe registers an indelible impression upon it. (Levi H. Dowling; 1980)[20]

Furthermore, a properly-trained esotericist is able to clairvoyantly access the akashic records, and thereby vividly investigate long-forgotten occurrences in the far-distant past. To be clear, akashic investigation is not some form of time travel; but simply accessing a detailed record of the past, analogous to viewing past events in a photo album.

Augmenting our conventional understanding of the Bible, the akashic investigations of Rudolf Steiner have surprisingly discovered that the gospels of St. Matthew and St. Luke refer to two different Jesus-families. While this unexpected esoteric information may be somewhat startling, disconcerting and unbelievable at first, discerning readers of St. Luke and St. Matthew will have already perceived that there are some noticeably-profound differences between these two gospels.

9.3 The Historical Co-Existence of Two Different Jesus-Families

For even casual students of the Bible, it is readily apparent that the genealogy of Jesus given in Chapter 1 of St.

THE DIFFERENT JESUS-FAMILIES IN ST. LUKE AND ST. MATTHEW

Matthew's gospel differs substantially from the genealogy given in Chapter 3 of St. Luke's gospel. In St. Matthew, Jesus descends from the Solomon line of King David; whereas in St. Luke, he descends from the Nathan line of King David.

This glaring difference could be easily explained away by simply concluding that one genealogy is correct and the other is incorrect. But if one believes in the inerrancy of the Bible, then a conclusion of error is not an option. In this case, clever theologians over the years have rationalized the two different genealogies by declaring that one applies to Joseph, the father of Jesus, and the other genealogy applies to Mary, the mother of Jesus.

The problem with this explanation is that ancient Hebrew society was patrilineal; that is, ancestral descent was determined by the male line, and not the female line. Because of this, both St. Matthew and St. Luke make a definite point of tracing Jesus' ancestry through Joseph. Mary is therefore not mentioned.

A further difficulty is the Western theological dogma of the "Miraculous Conception," the belief that Jesus did not have a biological father; but was instead supernaturally-conceived by the divine intervention of the Holy Spirit. If this was indeed the case, then why did the gospel writers bother to exactingly trace Jesus' biological genealogy through a step-father?

The akashic investigations of anthroposophical spiritual science reconciles the two different genealogies by boldly asserting that these apply to two different Josephs. Moreover, since there were two different Josephs, there were also two different Marys, and even more astounding—two different Jesus-children! In other words, at the same point in biblical history there co-existed two significant Hebrew families comprised of Joseph ("Yosef"), Mary ("Miryam") and Jesus ("Yeshua").

9.4 Different Family Accounts in the Gospel of St. Matthew and the Gospel of St. Luke

The esoteric assertion that there were two different Jesus-families described in the New Testament seems rather astounding and preposterous at first. But it turns out that Yosef, Miryam and Yeshua were very common names in biblical times. Having two co-existing families sharing these familiar Hebrew names back then would be as commonplace as finding two present-day families sharing the names of Joe, Mary and John (or Bill).

Moreover, there are other noticeable differences between the gospels of St. Matthew and St. Luke that clearly suggest the existence of two different Jesus-families. In St. Matthew, for example, sometime after Jesus was born the family was unexpectedly visited at their *house* in Bethlehem by three "wise men from the east." Soon after the wise men departed, the family surreptitiously fled to Egypt in order to avoid the murderous intent of King Herod. After the death of Herod, the family safely returned to Judea, and settled in Nazareth.

In St. Luke's gospel, however, prior to the birth of their Jesus-child, Mary and Joseph lived in Nazareth. They temporarily journeyed to Bethlehem in order to pay a compulsory Roman tax. Upon arrival, the local traveler's inn was already full, so Joseph and Mary were forced to stay elsewhere (according to tradition, in a nearby shepherd's cave). During the night, Mary gave birth to Jesus, "wrapped him in swaddling clothes, and laid him in a manger." Shortly after the birth, the family was visited by local shepherds who were angelically inspired to pay homage to the newborn child. According to Mosaic law, the Jesus-child was circumcised eight days after birth, and then presented to the temple priests in Jerusalem after 33 days. "And when they had performed all things according to the law of the Lord, they returned into Galilee, to their own city Nazareth" (Lk 2:39).

In the gospel of St. Luke, then, the family lives in Nazareth and not in Bethlehem; and there is no mention of three wise men nor an extended exile in Egypt.

There are also two conflicting beliefs regarding the size of the Jesus-family. According to Western theological dogma, Jesus was an only child; but according to certain biblical passages, Jesus had other brothers and sisters. The gospel of St. Matthew, for example, clearly states:

> Is not this the carpenter's son? Is not his mother called Mary? And are not his brethren James and Joseph and Simon and Judas? And are not all his sisters with us? (Matt 13:55, 56)

The notion that Jesus had other siblings has been traditionally explained away by asserting that these other relations were cousins, and not direct family members. Unfortunately, this convenient explanation is not supported by the fact that in biblical Greek, there are different words for "cousin" and "brother"; and the Greek word for cousin was not used in this particular passage.

Once again, the differences between the two Jesus-family accounts does not have to be a validity choice between one or the other. According to esoteric research, both family descriptions are quite correct: Jesus was an only child in the St. Luke family; but in the St. Matthew family, Jesus had other brothers and sisters.

CHAPTER 10:

THE "BLESSED VIRGIN MARY" OF ST. LUKE'S GOSPEL

10.1 The "Heavenly-Adam" and the "Heavenly-Eve"

EVEN THOUGH the New Testament contains no information about the birth and childhood of either gospel-Mary, an apocryphal writing known as "The Protoevangelium of James" (c.145 AD) contains a wealth of interesting background detail. While the early-childhood Marian events described in The Protoevangelium refer specifically to the Mary of St. Luke's gospel, the events surrounding the birth of Jesus are a descriptive composite of both St. Luke and St. Matthew.

According to the akashic research of spiritual science, the Mary-individual briefly indicated in St. Luke was a truly unique and special soul in world evolution. Soon after the gift of ego-consciousness was received in the ancient Lemurian Age, nascent humanity was covertly infiltrated by Luciferic evil. Theologically, this occurrence is referred to as "original sin." As a consequence of Luciferic interference, the once-immortal, ethereal forms of "paradisal" humanity that levitated high above the earth slowly densified (or "fell") into physical corporality. In other words, because of original sin, mankind began to inhabit bodies of flesh and blood that were subject to disease, deterioration and death; thereby necessitating the karmic process of rebirth and repeated embodiment.

The wise celestial overseers of mankind, however, (as preparation for the future) protected and preserved two ancestral souls—one male and one female—from Luciferic evil, and the consequent necessity to repeatedly inhabit dense corporeal bodies. Esoterically these two souls are known as the "heavenly-Adam" and the "heavenly-Eve."

Even though these two special human souls continued to exist throughout the ages in the uncorrupted, "virginal," angel-like condition that all of humanity had enjoyed before the "fall" into earthly mortality, they were not inactive or "quarantined" from the rest of humanity. Since the heavenly-Adam continued to experience an innate, atavistic unity with the universal masculine-principle, thereby retaining a primordial oneness of cosmic-being, he could act as a superphysical agent of spiritual inspiration for incarnated humanity. In this crucial, historical capacity, the heavenly-Adam acted as the spiritual inspiration behind such mythological figures as the Hindu Krishna and the Greek Apollo.

One the other hand, since the heavenly-Eve continued to experience an innate, atavistic unity with the universal feminine-principle, thereby retaining a primordial awareness of cosmic-consciousness, she could also act as a superphysical agent of spiritual inspiration for incarnated humanity. In this equally-crucial, historical capacity, the heavenly-Eve acted as the spiritual inspiration behind such mythological figures as the Egyptian Isis and the Greek Pallas Athena.

On numerous occasions, the heavenly-Eve was also

indwelt by a highly-advanced elohim-being—the spirit of the moon—biblically known as Yahweh.[21] Since Yahweh is the foremost representative of the Divine Mother for the Third Hierarchy of celestial beings, the heavenly-Eve has invisibly acted as a superphysical conduit of the Holy Spirit for incarnated mankind throughout the ages.

10.2 St. Luke's Mary: A "Virginal" Soul Without Previous Incarnations

According to esoteric investigation, it was the heavenly-Eve who physically incarnated for the very first time as the Mary-individuality described in St. Luke. Since the heavenly-Eve had been previously protected from Luciferic corruption, as St. Luke's Mary she was truly a "virgin-soul," born "immaculately-free" from the stain of original sin.

As a virgin-soul without prior physical incarnations, St. Luke's Mary had a boundless capacity for deep, intuitive understanding; and an all-embracing, kind, gentle and loving heart. However, without previous worldly experience, St. Luke's Mary displayed no aptitude for earthly-acquired skills, such as reading, writing, science, technology or arithmetic.

Mary's birth was considered to be a miracle by her elderly, previously-childless parents, Joachim and Anna. Moreover, they immediately understood that her pristine, innocent and delicate nature required specially-protective surroundings of purity and holiness. Consequently, for her first three years of mortal life, St. Luke's Mary was tenderly secluded and nurtured in Anna's bedchamber sanctuary, with assistance from specially-chosen, virginal handmaidens.

At three years of age, St. Luke's Mary was taken by her pious parents to the temple in Jerusalem, where she was joyously and unreservedly accepted as a consecrated temple virgin. As she had once been superphysically protected by advanced celestial-beings in various sacred sanctuaries prior to birth, St. Luke's Mary was raised and educated within the cloistered sanctuary of the Jerusalem temple until twelve years of age—the age of puberty. At this tender young age, she was betrothed by the high priest to a righteous, much older man named Joseph. As a kind and experienced father-figure, St. Luke's Joseph was able to provide St. Luke's Mary with paternal affection, care and material security.

At sixteen years of age, St. Luke's Mary conceived and gave birth to her one and only child, named Jesus. Though the child was conceived naturally, neither she nor Joseph consciously recalled any coital involvement, since conception occurred while both were in a somnambulant condition, similar to sleepwalking. In biblically terms, St. Luke's Mary truthfully declared: "How shall this be, seeing I *know* not a man?" (Lk 1:34).

This somnambulant state was induced by the action of etheric moon-forces which were particularly pronounced in St. Luke's Mary, due to the pre-incarnational indwelling of the lofty spirit of the moon. While this method of trance-like conception was highly exceptional at that time, it was once common practice for our primordial ancestors when they were still under the instinctual direction of a wise group-soul.[22]

Since the conception of St. Luke's Jesus-child was superphysically directed by the maternal moon-forces of Yahweh-elohim—the foremost representative of the Divine Mother for the Third Hierarchy—it can be esoterically stated that even though St. Luke's Joseph was the ("unknowing") biological father, St. Luke's Jesus was truly conceived by the actions of the Holy Spirit.

10.3 St. Luke's Jesus-Child: The Incarnation of the "Heavenly-Adam"

Rather astoundingly, the akashic research of spiritual science has also revealed that the Jesus-child born to St. Luke's Mary was the first physical incarnation of the heavenly-Adam. As was his beatific mother, then, St. Luke's Jesus was a "virgin-soul," born "immaculately-free" from all Luciferic corruption; that is, free from the injurious effects of original sin. Befittingly, in the cosmic scheme of development, the heavenly-Adam and the heavenly-Eve were together on earth as they had previously been united in the heavenly realms. Clearly the wise celestial overseers of mankind had foreseen, at the time of mankind's Luciferic "fall from grace," the necessity of two virginal-souls in the divine plan of salvation.

Soon after the Jesus-child of St. Luke was born in a Bethlehem cave, the holy family returned to Nazareth. Consonant with his mother, St. Luke's Jesus-child had no propensity for earthly-acquired talents; but did possess a boundless, universal compassion for all life. As described by Rudolf Steiner in a lecture given on 06 September 1910, and later published in *The Gospel of St. Matthew* (1985):

> The Nathan Jesus [described in St. Luke] developed with a strongly developed inward nature. While showing little aptitude for the acquisition of external wisdom, he possessed depth of soul and capacity for love in boundless measure, for dwelling in his etheric body was that force which had come down from a time before man's descent into earthly incarnation, when as yet he led a divine existence. Divinity dwelt in him in a boundless capacity for love. This Jesus of the Nathan line was little fitted for the acquisition of that which men gain in the course of incarnation in a physical body, but he was filled with an infinite warmth of love as regards his soul and inner being.

Under the protective watch and paternal care of St. Luke's

Joseph, mother and child grew together in domestic holiness as Mary schooled the tender soul of her son in the temple mysteries that she had once learned in Jerusalem. As well, Joseph tried patiently to instruct his otherworldly son in some of the practical skills of Hebrew life. Life in Nazareth was content and uneventful for St. Luke's holy family until the twelfth year of the Jesus-child's life. As related in St. Luke:

> Now his parents went to Jerusalem every year at the feast of the Passover. And when he was twelve years old, they went up according to custom … the boy Jesus stayed behind in Jerusalem … After three days they found him in the temple, sitting among the teachers, listening to them and asking them questions; and all who heard him were amazed at his understanding and his answers. And when they saw him they were astonished … And Jesus increased in wisdom and in stature, and in favor with God and man. (Lk 2:41–53)

The relieved but bewildered parents of the twelve-year-old Jesus-child were at a complete loss to understand how their big-hearted but simple-minded son had suddenly become a learned, cultured and erudite authority on deeply-religious ideas.

According to akashic research, when the twelve-year-old Jesus-child of St. Luke reached the stage of early-puberty, his still-virginal soul was permeated by the ego-forces of an illustrious bodhisattva-being.[23] This particular bodhisattva-being in a previous incarnation had been the original Zarathustra, the founder of the prehistoric Persian civilization. Since the Bodhisattva-Zarathustra had acquired immense wisdom, talent and ability through numerous significant incarnations (such as Zarathas, the teacher of Pythagoras), his indwelling influence on the soul of St. Luke's Jesus-child accounted for the startling transformation that occurred in the Jerusalem temple. The Bodhisattva-

Zarathustra continued to permeate and develop the soul of St. Luke's Jesus until the age of thirty, just prior to the baptism in the Jordan.[24]

10.4 The Predestined, Premature Death of St. Luke's Mary

Soon after the indwelling transformation of St. Luke's Jesus-child at the age of twelve, his fragile and delicate mother mysteriously wasted away and died from no apparent cause. To outward appearance, this was a shocking and tragic event. However, to esoteric insight, the withdrawal of St. Luke's Mary from the stage of worldly events at the tender age of 28 was destined to occur.

In the far-distant past, the rejuvenating etheric forces that maintain youthful vigor and health predominated until much later in human life. Unfortunately, over the centuries these regenerative forces became increasingly weaker, such that by the time of St. Luke's Mary, the degenerative forces of aging and debilitation were beginning to take hold between the young-adult years of 28 to 30.

Under normal circumstances, intellectual soul forces are activated at 28 to partially-counteract the aging process. In the case of St. Luke's Mary, however, since she had no prior physical incarnations, the forces of the intellectual soul had not been developed enough to sufficiently counteract the invasive forces of dissolution. Hence, the delicate form of St. Luke's Mary very quickly withered away, like a finely-cultivated rose without water. A similar fate would have befallen St. Luke's Jesus at the age of 30 if he hadn't been infused with the superplanetary forces of the Solar-Christos at the baptism.

St. Luke's Mary could have lived much longer with a similar soul infusion; but since her predestined mission on earth was accomplished, there was no need to extend her physical life. And that mission was to give birth to the heavenly-Adam on earth, and to prepare him up to the age of puberty for the later task of becoming the world messiah and saviour of mankind.

Even though St. John the Baptist was a powerful soul with numerous prior incarnations, he also submitted himself to an early death—in his case at the hands of King Herod—because his mission to prepare the way for the messiah was also accomplished. As he is quoted of saying: "I am not the Christ, but I have been sent before him ... He must increase, but I must decrease (Jn 3:28, 30).

10.5 The After-Death Existence of St. Luke's Mary as the "Blessed Virgin Mary"

Since the virginal soul of St. Luke's Mary remained immaculately free from Luciferic corruption at her death, she could dispense with any need for purgatorial purification on the other side. Moreover, she was able to very quickly regain the pristine, ethereal existence that she had enjoyed prior to physical incarnation; and thereby to radiantly revitalize her depleted virginal etheric-forces.

Even after death, St. Luke's Mary continued to remain superphysically connected to the crucial earthly events of her son Jesus. Simultaneous with the baptism of St. Luke's Jesus in the Jordan, for instance, she indwellingly permeated the soul of St. Matthew's Mary with her cosmically-revitalized virginal etheric-forces. Moreover, she continued to remain united with St. Matthew's Mary until her glorious assumption into heaven when she was 64 years old.

Since that time, St. Luke's Mary has made countless earthly appearances in etheric form to provide struggling humanity with crucial prophetic warnings, to contribute wise spiritual advice, to furnish solace and consolation, to administer comfort and healing, to sustain faith and hope, and to point the way to salvation through Christ-Jesus.

By continuing to remain immaculately-free from Luciferic corruption in an immortal "virginal" condition, St. Luke's Mary has come to be known throughout history as the "Blessed Virgin Mary." In fact, when she appeared to St. Bernadette at Lourdes in 1858, she declared: "I am the Immaculate Conception." Moreover, due to her selfless and compassionate service to humanity throughout the ages, and because of her great sacrifice to incarnate on earth in order to give birth and nurturance to the future messiah, the Blessed Virgin Mary has advanced to the level of an archangel; and can thereby pervade and protect entire nations on earth.

Moreover, together with great numbers of angel-ministrants, the Blessed Virgin Mary has made it her special mission to assist the seriously ill and the dying. Though largely unseen and unnoticed, she is at the bedside of the terminal, at the scene of human tragedy and natural disaster, and on the constant battlefield of warring nations.

Due to her pristine feminine nature, the Blessed Virgin Mary also superlatively embodies the cosmic principle of wisdom-sophia. As such, she is an especially-powerful conduit for the eternally-youthful healing-forces of the Holy Spirit-Mother—the Divine Sophia.

Since the beginning of the twentieth century, there have been more worldwide etheric apparitions of the Blessed Virgin Mary than during the entire preceding 1900 years.[25] This has been spiritually warranted to counteract the life-threatening tribulations on earth that occurred throughout the twentieth century: the rise of communism, two world wars, the development of atomic weaponry, and the Cold War battle between the USSR and the USA.

But additionally, the increased appearances of the Blessed Virgin Mary in the twentieth century have also been to herald the "second coming"; that is, to prepare mankind for the appearance of Christ-Jesus in etheric form, which began around 1933.

Figure 8: The Sacred Heart of the Blessed Virgin Mary

CHAPTER 11:

ST. MATTHEW'S MARY: THE "MOTHER OF THE WORLD"

11.1 The "Earthly-Adam" and the "Earthly-Eve"

THE AKASHIC RESEARCH of spiritual science recognizes a critical time in mankind's primordial past when there were only two human beings in existence on the entire earth—one male and one female. During the ancient Lemurian age, terrestrial conditions had become so inhospitable for human life, that only two human souls were strong enough to remain in physical existence. All others were temporarily forced to etherically exist on other planets in our solar system, such as Mars and Saturn. As described by Rudolf Steiner in a lecture given on 18 September 1909:

> During the Lemurian epoch there was actually a time when it may be said—with approximate accuracy at any rate—that there was a single couple in existence, *one main pair* which had retained sufficient strength to master the stubborn substance and to incarnate on the Earth, to 'hold out' as it were through the period when the Moon

was separating from the Earth. This separation made it possible again for human substance to be refined and rendered suitable to receive the weaker souls; the descendants of this one main pair were therefore able to live in more pliable substance than had been available before the separation of the Moon. Then, by degrees, all the souls returned to the Earth from Mars, Jupiter, Venus, Mercury and Saturn; and through propagation the souls gradually returning to the Earth from the planets constituted the descendants of the first main pair.

Esoterically, this primordial pair is known as the "earthly-Adam" and the "earthly-Eve." Both exceptional souls continued to incarnate throughout the ages as significant contributors to human development. The earthly-Adam soul, for instance, incarnated as the Old Testament Elijah, and later as St. John the Baptist. The earthy-Eve soul later incarnated as Mary, the mother of Jesus, in the gospel of St. Matthew.

11.2 St. Matthew's Mary: The Incarnation of the Earthly-Eve

As the incarnation of the earthly-Eve, St. Matthew's Mary possessed a calmly-steadfast inner nature, as well as a kind, maternal concern for others, especially those in need. Unlike St. Luke's Mary, St. Matthew's Mary needed no special care, safekeeping or guardianship. Through extensive incarnational experience, she had acquired a firm self-assurance and independent self-reliance. Moreover, she had a wealth of talent and ability that she kept mostly to herself, but which she easily drew on when any difficult situation arose.

While to date there has been very little esoteric investigation into her early life, St. Matthew's Mary is understood to have comfortably and uneventfully grown up in and around Bethlehem. In keeping with Hebrew marital custom, St. Matthew's Mary very likely married around the age of sixteen, and her husband Joseph around the age of 18. Their first-born child, Jesus—again according to Hebrew custom—was probably born during their first year of marriage.

As intimated in St. Matthew's gospel, this particular Jesus-child was born in a Bethlehem house, and not in a cave, some months prior to St. Luke's Jesus-child. It was the St. Matthew Jesus-child who attracted the attention of Persian magi because this child was also a very special incarnation; but one that was quite different from the incarnation of St. Luke's Jesus-child.

11.3 St. Matthew's Jesus-Child: The Incarnation of the Bodhisattva-Zarathustra

Whereas St. Luke's Jesus-child was a virgin soul without prior physical incarnations on earth, St. Matthew's Jesus-child was a highly-developed adept who had experienced extensive, illustrious incarnations on earth. In one of his most noteworthy embodiments he was known as Zarathustra ("Golden Star"), the founder of ancient Persian civilization.

As a highly-advanced initiate, the Zarathustra-individual has no further need to physically incarnate; but continues to do so out of selfless compassion for his fellow beings. As such, he is a "bodhisattva," and one of twelve such bodhisattva-beings belonging to the Great Mother-Lodge of Humanity who oversee the broad evolutionary development of all people on earth.

The incarnation of the Bodhisattva-Zarathustra as St. Matthew's Jesus-child naturally attracted the worldly attention of certain Persian Magi who clairvoyantly perceived the rebirth of their civilization's founder. By supersensibly following the astral light that radiated from the incarnation of the "Golden Star," three Persian magi were eventually led to the home of St. Matthew's Jesus-child in Bethlehem.

Intuiting the evil intention of King Herod to murder the recently-born Jesus-child, the magian priest-kings instructed the holy family to take refuge in Egypt, and to not return until after the death of Herod. To financially assist in the costly burden of travelling and relocating to a foreign land, the magi helpfully provided St. Matthew's Jesus-family with gold, frankincense and myrrh. Fortunately, St. Luke's Jesus-family was spared the need to take similar foreign refuge, since their Jesus-child was born after Herod massacred all the infants in Bethlehem.

Not surprisingly, since St. Matthew's Jesus was the incarnation of an exalted bodhisattva, he was a very precocious child from the very beginning, exhibiting a wealth of talent, ability and profound knowledge. As described by Rudolf Steiner in a lecture given on 17 December 1913:

> And so the [St. Matthew] Jesus-boy ... in whom lived the Ego of Zarathustra, was endowed with faculties of a very high order. They made it easy for him to understand what was present in his environment as the fruits of the culture achieved by humanity on Earth through the various epochs. In the environment of such a child—especially in former times—the whole culture of mankind was embodied in sacred rituals, in worship, in ceremonial enactments. An ordinary child takes in little of what he sees and hears. But this boy assimilated with great inner genius, from the sparsest indications, what had been achieved by humanity. In short, he evinced a supreme gift for absorbing the scholarship and learning produced by culture hitherto. Such a child today would be called "highly gifted". Up to his twelfth year this [St. Matthew's] Jesus-boy rapidly assimilated everything that could be learnt from his environment. (Published in *The Fifth Gospel*; 1985)

After the death of Herod, St. Matthew's Jesus-family safely returned to Palestine, but resettled in Nazareth instead of Bethlehem. By the time the St. Matthew Jesus-boy was twelve years old, he had four younger brothers: James, Joses, Judas and Simon; and two younger sisters: Mary and Salome.

11.4 The Predestined, Premature Death of St. Matthew's Jesus-Boy

For a time, St. Matthew's Jesus-family lived comfortably and happily in Nazareth, in close proximity to St. Luke's Jesus-family. But it wasn't long before tragedy struck both Jesus-families. Shortly before the twelfth birthday of St. Matthew's Jesus-boy, his young father became ill and suddenly died. If that wasn't tragedy enough for St. Matthew's Mary, her special Jesus-boy also died suddenly soon after his twelfth birthday.

To ordinary observation, the sudden death of St. Matthew's Jesus-boy could have seemed a cruel and senseless blow of fate, or a vicious attack by the powers of darkness. But to esoteric investigation, the premature death of the St. Matthew Jesus-boy was predestined to occur.

It was never intended by the divinely-inspired overseers of mankind that the St. Matthew Jesus-boy would live to adulthood; but instead, that he would indwell the St. Luke Jesus-boy at puberty in order to strengthen and prepare his delicately-refined body and soul to become the messiah. By permeating St. Luke's Jesus-boy with the powerful ego-forces of the Bodhisattva-Zarathustra until the age of thirty, a solid psycho-somatic foundation would be established to receive the powerful superplanetary forces of the Solar-Christos (the "Christ") at the pre-destined baptism in the Jordan.

Sadly, none of this pre-destined preparation was consciously understood by the grief-stricken Mary of St.

Matthew. Having lost her dear husband and first-born son, for a dark but thankfully brief time St. Matthew's Mary was left alone to raise six children in Nazareth. But as the incarnation of the earthly-Eve, St. Matthew's Mary had an incredibly strong and resilient nature; and therefore never faltered or hesitated in her duties as a protective and caring mother.

11.5   The Two Jesus-Families of Nazareth Become One

As previously mentioned in Chapter 10, soon after the bodhisattvic-indwelling that dramatically transformed St. Luke's twelve-year-old Jesus-boy in the Jerusalem temple, St. Luke's Mary suddenly passed away. That left St. Luke's Joseph on his own in Nazareth to raise his unusual Jesus-son.

Since both Jesus-families were familiar neighbours in Nazareth, it was somewhat predictable (as well as pre-destined) that after the seeming tragedies that befell both families, they would join together for mutual survival and benefit. St. Matthew's Mary, then, by a complex twist of destiny, regained her own deceased Jesus-son now inwardly permeating the soul of her new step-son, St. Luke's Jesus-boy.

At first, St. Matthew's Mary did not recognize that the precocious ego-forces shining through St. Luke's Jesus-boy originated from her departed son. Nevertheless, as time went by, she and St. Luke's Jesus-boy grew closer and closer in love and understanding; to the point that she considered her step-son to be her very own.

11.6   The Profound Inner Transformations of St. Matthew's Mary

According to esoteric research, the evening prior to his baptism in the Jordan at the age of 30, St. Luke's Jesus had an especially intimate conversation with St. Matthew's Mary in the home of Lazarus. As St. Luke's Jesus spoke, the ego-forces of the Bodhisattva-Zarathustra slowly withdrew from his soul vehicles, and then passed through the receptive soul vehicles of St. Matthew's Mary. In doing so, these departing forces left a lasting imprint of the entire life-experience of the Bodhisattva-Zarathustra on the soul of St. Matthew's Mary.

In addition to the exuding ego-forces of the Bodhisattva-Zarathustra that were imprinted on the soul of St. Matthew's Mary the night before, at the exact moment that the Solar-Christos entered the soul of St. Luke's Jesus at the baptism, the powerfully-revitalized etheric-forces of St. Luke's Mary (who had deceased 18 years earlier) simultaneously entered the soul of St. Matthew's Mary as well. This had the transformative effect of completely restoring the pre-pubescent etheric-forces of youthful revitalization and health. In other words, in connection with her etheric body, St. Matthew's Mary—at the age of 46—was restored to the "virginal" condition that she experienced prior to adolescence.[26]

As Rudolf Steiner explained in a lecture given on 3 July 1909 entitled "What Occurred at the Baptism?":

> The moment when the Spirit of Christ descended into the body of Jesus of Nazareth and the transformation already described took place, an effect was wrought also upon the mother of Jesus of Nazareth. This effect consisted in the circumstance that in the instant of the Baptism by John she regained her state of virginhood: that is to say, her inner organism reverted to the condition of the feminine organism before maidenly puberty. At the birth of Christ the mother of Jesus of Nazareth became Virgin (due to the transformation of her inner organs to the state in which they existed prior to her puberty).

ST. MATTHEW'S MARY: THE "MOTHER OF THE WORLD"

After St. Luke's Jesus was baptized by St. John the Baptist, St. Matthew's Mary immediately noticed a profound change in her step-son. He began to speak and act with great power and authority; and soon began to perform amazing miracles everywhere he went. Though St. Matthew's Mary did not understand at first that St. Luke's Jesus was indwelt by the Solar-Christos at the baptism—and is henceforth known as "Christ-Jesus"—she had no doubts that by some mysterious process he had become the "promised messiah" and the "saviour of mankind."

By unquestioningly embracing her messiah-son's every word and deed, St. Matthew's Mary underwent a profound, subconscious initiatory development. By faithfully following her Christed-son to the foot of the cross, St. Matthew's Mary empathetically shared in the agonizing events of his mystic death, as well as his triumphant resurrection and ascension. Moreover, at Pentecost, St. Matthew's Mary was especially permeated with the divine-forces of the Holy Mother-Spirit that issued from the superplanetary spirit-self of the Risen Christ.

After the ascension of Christ-Jesus, St. Matthew's Mary was cared for by St. John the Beloved, as he was instructed to do at the cross. According to the visions of Blessed Anne Catherine Emmerich (1774–1824), St. Matthew's Mary "lived for three years on Mount Sion, for three years in Bethany, and for nine years in Ephesus."

At the age of 64, in her stone house nearby Ephesus, and surrounded by a number of apostles, the radiant soul of St. Matthew's Mary gloriously ascended into heaven. Her body was place in a small nearby cave that had been prepared as a sepulcher. Once again referring to Blessed Anne Catherine Emmerich, the bodily assumption of St. Matthew's Mary occurred on the same night that she had died. In Sister Emmerich's own words:

> In the night I saw several of the Apostles and holy

women praying and singing in the little garden in front of the rock-tomb. A broad shaft of light came down from heaven to the rock, and I saw descending in it a triple-ringed glory of angels and spirits surrounding the appearance of Our Lord and of the shining soul of Mary ... As this vision, becoming ever clearer, streamed down upon the rock, I saw a shining path opened and leading up to the heavenly Jerusalem. Then I saw the soul of the Blessed Virgin, which had been following the appearance of Jesus, pass in front of Him, and float down into the tomb. Soon afterwards I saw her soul, united to her transfigured body, rising out of the tomb far brighter and clearer, and ascending into the heavenly Jerusalem with Our Lord and with the whole glory. Thereupon all the radiance faded again, and the quiet starry sky covered the land.

11.7 The After-Death Existence of St. Matthew's Mary as "Blessed Mary, the Mother of the World"

Spiritual science concurs with Western theology that the only two individuals who have successfully resurrected the physical human form are Christ-Jesus and Blessed Mary. As succinctly stated by Rudolf Steiner in a lecture given on 11 February 1906 entitled "The Medieval View of the World in Dante's Divine Comedy":

> Only the Christ and Mary were able to take their bodies into the fixed star heaven ...
>
> Jesus and Mary had hallowed their physical body to such a degree that they were able to take it with them to the highest regions.

Because of her immense contribution to humanity throughout the ages as the earthly-Eve, and due to the profound and accelerated initiatory development that she underwent in connection with the life of Christ-Jesus on earth, St. Matthew's Mary has also advanced to the level of an archangel. In association with Christ-Jesus and the twelve bodhisattvas in Shambhala who constitute the inner government of the world, St. Matthew's Mary has assumed the office of world-mother (referred to in the East as the "Jagat-Amba"). As such, she is better referred to as "Blessed Mother Mary" or "Blessed Mary, the Mother of the World."

In mankind's primordial, undeveloped past, the offices of the inner government were occupied by wise beings far in advance of ordinary humanity (primarily by archangelic beings from the sphere of Mercury). As mankind progressed in spiritual development, these positions have become filled by highly-advanced human initiates. Prior to Blessed Mother Mary, the office of world-mother was occupied by the archangelic being (goddess) known in the East as Guanshiyin ("She who hears the cries of the world": see Figure 9). In other words, Blessed Mother Mary is the first human initiate to occupy the office of world-mother (see Figure 10) .

As world-mother, Blessed Mother Mary embraces the concerns of every woman in the world, particularly those who are mothers. Moreover, together with vast numbers of angel-attendants at her direction, Blessed Mother Mary is superphysically involved at every stage of child-birth and child-rearing. Whereas the Blessed Virgin Mary compassionately ministers to those souls who are exiting mortal existence, Blessed Mother Mary compassionately ministers to those souls entering mortal existence. As expressed by Theosophist and clairvoyant Geoffrey Hodson in *The Brotherhood of Angels and of Men* (2011):

> [The World-Mother] labours ever for the cause of human motherhood, and even now is bending all Her mighty strength and calling all Her Angel court to labour for the upliftment of motherhood throughout the world.

Through Her Angel messengers She Herself is present at every human birth—unseen and unknown, it is true, but if men would open their eyes She would be revealed.

Figure 9: Guanshiyin as "The Giver of Children"

Figure 10: Blessed Mary, the "Mother of the World"

CHAPTER 12:

MYTHS AND MISCONCEPTIONS ABOUT WISDOM-SOPHIA

12.1 The Heavenly-Sophia is not the Same as the Divine-Sophia

IT'S IMPORTANT TO BE esoterically clear that there is only one complete and perfect personification of wisdom-sophia in reality, and that is the Divine Sophia, the Holy Mother-Person of the Blessed Trinity. Her highest reflection in the created universe—that is, within the Logos-Word—is the universal feminine-principle, or heavenly-sophia. The heavenly-sophia, then, is not a separate and distinct celestial-being (or "goddess"); but rather, the "feminine side" or the "maternal nature" of the one universal-life that is the Logos-Word.

All human and celestial life-forms are unique and independent likenesses of the one universal-life; and therefore incorporate universal-wisdom (heavenly-sophia) and universal-being to various degrees. In other words, even though heavenly-sophia is not a personified celestial-entity, she is embodied in every life-form throughout the vast cosmos.

To erroneously believe that heavenly-sophia is an independent celestial-entity within the universe, is equivalent to a human person declaring that the universal-wisdom, which is limitedly embodied within them as well, is also a separate entity.

12.2   There is no Such Thing as the "Triple Goddess"

The modern neo-pagan and neo-wiccan belief in a "Triple Goddess" who manifests as maiden, mother and crone has no basis in spiritual reality. As all true esotericists will attest (and confirmed by basic logic), a divine-being that is eternal cannot experience the decline and debilitation of old-age. A feminine divine-being, then, could never become an old "crone."

The experience of old-age only applies to human beings ensouled in dense material bodies that are subject to chemical disintegration and decomposition. Prior to the Lemurian "fall" into physical materiality, human forms were immortal and not subject to illness, decay, injury or death.

Likewise, superphysical celestial beings (such as angels, archangels and seraphim) have no experience of old-age or death; they undergo a continual process of metamorphosis and renewal.

The Divine Sophia, as the feminine-person of the Holy Trinity, personifies the divine forces of eternal creation; and is, therefore, eternally young and forever pristine. The feminine substance of the Divine Sophia eternally fluctuates from "virginal" potentiality to "maternal" manifestation. The Divine Sophia (or Holy Spirit), therefore, is *both* virgin and mother. In divine reality, she can never be "crone."

Moreover, the rationale that the three stages of the Triple

Goddess conform to the "three phases of the moon"—two crescents and a full moon—is entirely contrived. As we all know, there are two major lunar phases: new moon and full moon; four principal lunar phases new moon, first quarter, full moon and third quarter; and four intermediate lunar phases: waxing crescent, waxing gibbous, waning gibbous and waning crescent. Arbitrarily choosing two crescents and a full moon entirely ignores the fact of the new moon.

Moreover, claiming that the three aspects of the Triple Goddess—maiden, mother and crone—conform to the stages in a woman's life is also artificially incomplete. A better representation would be newborn, maiden, mother, crone and corpse. The three stages of the Triple Goddess ignores the crucial stages of birth and death, which would correspond with the new moon.

The characteristic nature of the Divine Sophia (Holy Spirit) as both virgin and mother better conforms to the major phases of the moon—the new moon and the full moon. The new moon corresponds to the virginal "newness" of divine feminine substance prior to inception; and the full moon corresponds to the maternal "fullness" of procreation after inception.

Even though the Divine Sophia is both virginal and maternal, each of the two New Testament Marys best embodies one of these dual attributes (even though they each include both). The Blessed Virgin Mary obviously exemplifies the virginal nature of the Holy Spirit to a supernal degree; while Blessed Mother Mary obviously exemplifies the maternal nature of the Holy Spirit to a supernal degree.

12.3 The Blessed Virgin Mary is not Anthropo-Sophia

It is very unfortunate that in the present day there are a great many authors who write with such "esoteric" authority and conviction, but who have had little or no direct spiritual experience about what they write. Predictably, the information they convey with such weight and command is rife with error and falsehood.

Perhaps nowhere is this more apparent than when they emphatically expound on the "being" of anthropo-sophia. If these pseudo-authorities had actually experienced the "lesser guardian of the threshold" for themselves, they would have a much clearer understanding of what Rudolf Steiner means by the "being" of anthropo-sophia.

For those who may be unfamiliar, the lesser guardian is a fearful astral figure that is objectively materialized out of an individual's collective karma; that is, out of the accumulated effects of good and bad deeds that were performed throughout an individual's incarnational history. The lesser guardian is invisible to ordinary sight; and only becomes visible to supersensible sight when an individual attempts to consciously cross the threshold into the spiritual world. The lesser guardian, then, is a spectral apparition, a personal astral creation. As figuratively described by Rudolf Steiner in Chapter 10 of *Knowledge of the Higher Worlds and its Attainment* (1986):

> But now all the good and evil sides of thy bygone lives shall be revealed to thee. Hitherto they were interwoven with thine own being; they were in thee and thou couldst not see them, even as thou canst not behold thine own brain with physical eyes. But now they become released from thee; they detach themselves from thy personality. They assume an independent form which thou canst see even as thou beholdest the stones and plants of the outer world. And . . . I am that very being who shaped my body out of thy good and evil achievements. My spectral form is woven out of thine own life's record.

It will be gathered from the above that the Guardian of

the Threshold is an (astral) figure, revealing itself to the student's awakened higher sight ...

So, if the lesser guardian is simply an astral materialization of accumulated karma, why does Steiner refer to it as "that very being" in the above quotation (and elsewhere)? The reason is to disclose and emphasize the supersensible fact that objective materializations in the astral world which issue from human activity are more than just ephemeral, inanimate creations that quickly disappear without effect.

Instead, these astral materializations will often assume a distinct human-like form; and being composed of astral substance, they possess a certain vitality as well as a degree of elemental mentation and sentience. Moreover, these humanly-generated astral formations will very often detach themselves from their human creator, and lead an independent existence in astral space; thereby affecting other astral formations in the superphysical environment.

While it's important to recognize that astral materializations such as the lesser guardian exhibit a "being-like" quality of existence, it's equally important to understand that these being-like astral formations are not "beings" in the usually-understood sense of existing as spirit-filled "persons," such as human beings and celestial beings. An astral materialization such as the lesser guardian does not possess an organized assemblage of interpenetrating body and soul vehicles, such as an etheric body or an intellectual soul. Nor is the divine nature reflected in these astral materializations as an individualized spiritual-self. Moreover, a being-like astral creation does not have an extensive evolutionary history belonging to a particular life-wave, such as the angels, or the archangels, or the thrones or the seraphim.

From what has been described, then, it is clear that anthropo-sophia is a "being-like" astral materialization, and not a "being" in the same sense as a "human being," as an ego-indwelt human "person." Even though cosmic wisdom-sophia is as old as the universe, anthropo-sophia is only a recent manifestation.

Anthropo-sophia is essentially an objective materialization of spiritual-truth (cosmic wisdom-sophia) that has been consciously acquired by the human intellect through spiritual scientific means. As such, she only came into existence with the establishment of anthroposophical spiritual science by Rudolf Steiner in the early 1900s. Anthropo-sophia began as a personal materialization of the spiritual-truth acquired by Steiner himself; somewhat similar to the personal generation of the lesser guardian. But as more and more of his pupils began to apply the techniques of spiritual science to intellectually acquire spiritual truth as well, anthropo-sophia very quickly transformed from being a *personal* astral materialization, into becoming a *collective* one.

Since cosmic wisdom-sophia is a universal feminine-principle, the human-like form assumed by anthropo-sophia is predictably a feminine one. Moreover, even though she only recently came into materialized existence, she assumes the form of a "mature" woman due to the tremendous outpouring of spiritual truth that was acquired and conveyed by Steiner himself. As more and more individuals intellectually acquire cosmic wisdom-truth through spiritual science, anthropo-sophia naturally increases in astral stature, beauty, strength and influence. Moreover, as an astral "being-like" manifestation, anthropo-sophia is imbued with a degree of vitality, sentience and mentation.

Given that anthropo-sophia has only recently come into astral existence, it is somewhat perplexing why some anthroposophical writers have erroneously suggested that the Blessed Virgin Mary (of St. Luke's gospel) and anthropo-sophia are one and the same being. As recognized by spiritual science, the Blessed Virgin Mary was the first and only physical incarnation of the heavenly-Eve. Since the heavenly-Eve has been a part of human evolution since its very inception, she is a human "being" in the fullest sense of the term, and is not a "being-like" astral materialization like anthropo-sophia..

What is equally perplexing is the assertion by some anthroposophical writers that the heavenly-Eve is not an actual human being but simply a pristine aspect of the earthly-Eve's etheric body that was preserved from Luciferic corruption (and the resultant "fall" into physical incarnation) during ancient Lemurian times. If this were true, then the incarnation of the heavenly-Eve as St. Luke's Mary is nothing but the physical embodiment of an uncorrupted etheric body-fragment.

According to this ill-conceived notion, then, the immaculate mother of St. Luke's Jesus-child would have had no individualized soul or indwelling spirit. As such, she would have been a plant and not a human being! On strictly logical grounds, then, the idea that the heavenly-Eve is simply preserved etheric forces is obviously absurd. If these pseudo-esoteric authorities had taken the time to combine *all* that Rudolf Steiner revealed concerning the heavenly-Adam, they would have a correct understanding of the heavenly-Eve.

What is strangely ironic in this instance is the fact that it is usually the same self-styled esoteric authorities who claim that the heavenly-Eve—a real human being—is nothing but an etheric materialization, who also assert that anthropo-sophia—an astral materialization—is a real human being! As previously mentioned, this confusion on their part is a clear indication that they "know not of what they speak"; and should therefore keep esoterically silent.

12.4 Sophia is not the Feminine Counterpart to Christ

First introduced by gnostic writers in the early years of Christianity is the erroneous notion that Christ and Sophia are cosmic complementaries: male/female pairs—a kind of celestial marital-couple. Sophia is often referred to as the "bride of Christ." In the exotic language of Gnosticism, they are known as "aeon syzygies."

To begin with, there is no marriage in heaven, no gendered-pairing of celestial beings. As Christ-Jesus is quoted as saying: "For in the resurrection they neither marry nor are given in marriage, but are like angels in heaven" (Matt 20:30). However, every human and celestial being—including the Logos-Word—is a reflection of the Divine Trinity; and therefore includes both masculine and feminine qualities. Every celestial being is gender-combined, and therefore requires no additional celestial being for gender balance and complementarity.

The one divine nature of God is also a perfect pairing of masculine-being (the heavenly Father) and feminine-wisdom (the Holy Mother). The one God does not require a divine "Goddess" for gender balance either. Within the one divine nature, then, the gender complement to the Divine Sophia is the Heavenly Father, not the Eternal Son. The Eternal Son is the perfect unity of the Heavenly Father and the Holy Mother (the Divine Sophia).

"Christ" as we know from spiritual science is a highly-advanced archangelic being, better referred to as the "Solar-Christos"—the exalted regent of the sun. As advanced as he is, the Christ-being is certainly not equally "paired-up" with the Divine Sophia, one of the Trinitarian persons of God. Nor is the Christ-being on an equal footing with the heavenly-sophia, the feminine aspect of the Logos-Word, the one universal-person.

In short, the Christ-being requires no celestial counterpart for gender balance. As for "Sophia," the heavenly-sophia (or universal feminine-principle) is complemented by the universal masculine-principle; and the Divine Sophia (or Holy Mother) is complemented by the Heavenly Father. Neither is complemented by the Christ-being.

12.5 The Coming "Age of Sophia" is a Luciferic Distraction

There's an erroneous notion being bandied about by certain sophia-proponents that cosmic wisdom-sophia (as the "goddess Sophia") is slowly descending from her distant celestial abode and drawing ever-closer to truth-starved mankind. Moreover, the next cultural era of Western civilization is being described as the "Age of Sophia," as the coming goddess of wisdom increasingly permeates eager human minds. While all this sounds quite celebratory, it actually runs completely counter to true cognitive development for mankind.

According to spiritual science, the next post-Atlantean cultural era will begin in 3573 and last until 5733. Rudolf Steiner gave various descriptive names to this cultural era: the "Slavic age," the "age of the spirit-self," and the "age of Aquarius." Nowhere in his writings did he use the term, "age of Sophia." This descriptor is clearly a recently-contrived one.

Furthermore, the notion that the goddess Sophia is descending from cosmic heights and increasingly approaching mankind on earth is entirely anachronistic, and completely contravenes the actual practice and significance of anthroposophical spiritual science.

During mankind's primordial past, cosmic wisdom-truth streamed into passive human souls from the starry periphery in the form of dream-like revelations. To rudimentary clairvoyant vision, this cosmic wisdom-truth assumed the astral appearance of an archangel, such as the Egyptian goddess-figure, Isis. Over time, as mankind began to develop abstract intellectual thought, cosmic wisdom-truth gradually faded from human experience, and was replaced by the empirical knowledge of the physical, material world. In its early stages, this vibrant, newly-conceivable worldly-wisdom was imaginatively visualized as a beautiful angel-figure, such as Lady Philosophia. As intellectual thought gradually become more and more materialistic and secular, all imaginative personifications of knowledge disappeared entirely.

With the establishment of anthroposophical spiritual science by Rudolf Steiner, intellectual thinking was directed away from the chemical, material world and refocused on the spiritual world. By employing the methodology and techniques of spiritual science, intellectual thought reaches out to the spiritual world, and cosmic wisdom-truth is thereby obtained in a self-directed, fully-conscious way.

In other words, beginning with the modern age and continuing into the future, cosmic wisdom-truth (heavenly-sophia) is not coming towards humanity; humanity is intellectually reaching out to universal wisdom-sophia. As occurs with a mirror, when one reaches out towards the surface of the mirror, the reflected image appears to be coming back towards the viewer. Similarly in the spiritual world, wisdom-sophia only *appears* to coming toward humanity.

Moreover, the collective spiritual truth (wisdom-sophia) that individual human beings have intellectually acquired through spiritual science astrally materializes in the form of a radiantly-beautiful human female, known esoterically as "anthropo-sophia." Once again, rather than coming towards mankind, anthropo-sophia leads mankind out into the spiritual world in order to particularly gain increased wisdom-truth regarding the saviour of mankind, Christ-Jesus. Without intellectually acquiring the necessary spiritual truth (wisdom-sophia) concerning Christ-Jesus, mankind will not be able to manifest the divine forces required to properly continue human evolution on earth.

Intellectually acquiring cosmic wisdom-truth through

anthroposophical spiritual science also rescues heavenly-sophia from the clutches of Luciferic distortion and exaggeration. In fact, esoteric dilettantes need to be aware that Lucifer, as a fallen-away spirit of wisdom, will attempt to deceive the unwary by posing as the radiant goddess Sophia. But in the case of Lucifer, what is radiated is a false wisdom-light that glows with selfishness, egotism and pride.

To fervently maintain that the heavenly-sophia is presently descending towards mankind from out of the starry regions is clearly a regressive return to the past. And as all seasoned esotericists know, any improper attempt to divert attention to the past, or to revive the outmoded conditions of the past, is a Luciferic impulse that will only result in ruination and despair.

It can also be easily concluded that focusing esoteric attention on an imaginary "coming of Sophia" is a Luciferically-inspired distraction from the real "second coming of Christ-Jesus" in etheric form that is intended to happen from now into the next cultural era.[27]

12.6 The "Virgin Sophia" is not Simply the Purified Consciousness Soul

Some unfortunate confusion regarding wisdom–sophia has resulted from symbolically using macrocosmic and historical beings and events to describe microcosmic, intra-psychic activity and development. As experienced esotericists have learned concerning major evolutionary events, what often occurs externally on the large stage of world history will later take place internally on the intimate stage of the human soul.

Not surprisingly, then, the world-transforming events potentially affecting all mankind that resulted from the incarnational life of Christ-Jesus are divinely intended to have a life-transformative effect within the souls of individual human beings as well.

In the case of external historical events, it was necessary that the immaculate, virginal soul of the heavenly-Eve incarnate as St. Luke's Mary, and to be permeated with the divine-maternal forces of the Holy Spirit in order to give birth to the saviour of the world. Similarly, it was necessary for the soul of St. Luke's Jesus to be permeated by the ego-forces of the Bodhisattva-Zarathustra as preparation to endure the powerful descent of the Holy Spirit at the baptism, which enabled the indwelling presence of the Solar-Christos (the Christ).

On a much more modest level within the individual human soul, it is necessary to purify the consciousness soul (symbolically represented by the Virgin Mary-Sophia) in order to properly unfold the germinal "spirit-self" vehicle of expression (which is particularly suffused with the spirit-forces of the Holy Spirit—see Figure 11 on the following page).

Once the spirit-self vehicle of spiritual consciousness has been sufficiently developed, it is able to give birth to "life-spirit," the vehicle of cosmic consciousness that is particularly suffused with the spirit-forces of the Eternal Son. Moreover, since Christ-Jesus was the first being on earth to unfold the germinal vehicle of life-spirit, the consciousness pertaining to this vehicle has also been termed, "Christ consciousness."

On the stage of world history Christ-Jesus declared: "No one comes to the Father except through Me" (Jn 14:6); and "He who has seen Me has seen the Father" (Jn 14:9). Within the soul of individual human beings these statements are interpreted to mean that the unfoldment of the "spirit-body" vehicle of divine consciousness is only possible when the Son-imbued vehicle of life-spirit is sufficiently developed.

COSMIC REALMS OF EXISTENCE	INDIVIDUAL LEVELS OF EXISTENCE	VEHICLES OF EXPRESSION	EGO (SELF)	BIBLICAL SYMBOLISM	DEGREES OF CONSCIOUSNESS
CELESTIAL WORLD [SPIRIT LAND]	SPIRIT	SPIRIT-BODY	THE HIGHER EGO (SELF)	THE HEAVENLY FATHER	DIVINE CONSCIOUSNESS
		LIFE-SPIRIT		THE ETERNAL SON	COSMIC CONSCIOUSNESS
		SPIRIT-SELF		THE HOLY SPIRIT	SPIRITUAL CONSCIOUSNESS
SOUL WORLD	SOUL	CONSCIOUSNESS SOUL	THE LOWER EGO (SELF)	THE VIRGIN MARY-SOPHIA	SOUL CONSCIOUSNESS
		INTELLECTUAL SOUL		MARY, WIFE OF CLEOPHAS	SELF CONSCIOUSNESS
		SENTIENT SOUL		MARY MAGDALENE	WAKING CONSCIOUSNESS
	BODY	ASTRAL BODY			DREAM CONSCIOUSNESS
PHYSICAL WORLD		ETHERIC BODY			SLEEP CONSCIOUSNESS
		PHYSICAL BODY			TRANCE CONSCIOUSNESS

Figure 11: Biblical Symbolism and Vehicles of Expression

While the foregoing should be clear and straightforward to most esotericists, unfortunately some sophia-proponents have muddied the intellectual waters by intimating that the consciousness soul *is* the Virgin Sophia; instead of correctly stating that the purified consciousness soul is symbolically *represented* by the Virgin Sophia; or that the purified consciousness soul is *imbued* with the virginal forces of the Divine Sophia.

Furthermore, the purified consciousness soul can also be accurately and meaningfully represented by St. John the Baptist, since he also comes before the Messiah to prepare the way, and to purify the receptive-soul through baptism and repentance. Another accurate biblical symbol for the purified consciousness soul is St. Michael the archangel, since he annually purifies the sulphurized autumnal atmosphere of the earth as planetary preparation for the descent of Christ-Jesus (as planetary-spirit) to the heart of the earth, and the consequent birth of the new year at the winter solstice.

12.7 The Gospel of St. John is not Literally the "Virgin Sophia"

A clear and concise understanding of "Sophia" has also been obscured by taking certain statements made by Rudolf Steiner in connection with the Gospel of St. John far too literally. Take for example the following quotation from a lecture given on 25 November 1907 entitled "Sophia is the Gospel Itself":

> The spiritualized mother of Jesus is the Gospel itself. She is wisdom, leading humanity to the highest insights. The disciple [St. John the Evangelist] gave us Mother Sophia, meaning he wrote a Gospel for us that allows anyone who looks into it to learn to know Christ, who is the

source and goal of this great movement (spiritual science).

Obviously St. John's gospel is not some sort of compressed physical incarnation of the entire ocean of cosmic wisdom-sophia. Nevertheless, this special gospel was certainly directly inspired by cosmic wisdom-sophia and certainly conveys profound spiritual truth. As such, St. John's gospel is more than just an ordinary written account of the life of Christ-Jesus.

Esoterically, it is an initiatory guide-book that can lead to an authentic encounter with the Risen Christ who is able to completely transform our spiritual lives. As further stated by Rudolf Steiner in the lecture, "The Nature of the Virgin Sophia and of the Holy Spirit" (May 1908):

> By continually meditating upon passages of the Gospel of St. John, students of Christian initiation are actually in a condition to reach initiation without the three-and-a-half-day continued lethargic sleep [of the ancient Mysteries] … John's Gospel is not there simply to be read and understood with the intellect; it must be fully experienced and felt inwardly. It is a force that aids and works for initiation.

In other words, St. John's gospel is not literally the "Virgin Sophia"; but rather an initiatory document *shaped* by cosmic wisdom-sophia that *contains* sublime sophia-truth concerning Christ-Jesus.

CONCLUSION

DESPITE ALL THE present-day confusion and misinformation about who or what is "Sophia," it should be clear from the foregoing detailed examination that there is only one perfect personification of divine wisdom-truth and that is the Trinitarian-person of the Holy Spirit-Mother, esoterically known as the Divine Sophia. There is no Triple Goddess, no Feminine Trinity, and no Aeon Sophia.

Logically, there can be only one perfect personification of wisdom-sophia, and that is within the eternal and infinite personhood of God. Within creation, all beings—human and celestial—imperfectly reflect the Holy Trinity, including the spiritual wisdom of the Divine Sophia. Within creation, there is no being who exclusively personifies wisdom-sophia. All persons within the created universe (the Logos-Word) incorporate to various degrees the feminine-principle of wisdom-truth, and the masculine-principle of being-identity.

During the distant prehistoric past, cosmic wisdom-truth—the feminine-principle of the Logos-Word—was conveyed to human beings in the form of dream-like clairvoyant pictures. Unfortunately, surreptitious Luciferic forces in the human soul increasingly distorted, corrupted and concealed cosmic wisdom-truth. In time, and due to the additional influence of Ahrimanic materialism, human access to undefiled spiritual truth would have disappeared entirely if it weren't for the incarnational intervention of divine forces through Christ-Jesus.

In consequence of the transformative activity of Christ-Jesus within earthly evolution, Rudolf Steiner was able to establish anthroposophical spiritual science as a modern method of intellectually accessing spiritual wisdom-truth. Through anthroposophy, then, human beings are able to overcome Luciferic interference, and once again perceive the glory of the Divine Sophia reflected in the universal wisdom that permeates the entire cosmos.

Certain advanced beings superlatively embody the spiritual forces of the Holy Spirit, the Divine Sophia. In traditional Christian theology, the foremost human being to be "filled with the grace" of the Holy Spirit is recognized to be Mary, the mother of Jesus. But as we surprisingly learn from the akashic research of spiritual science, there are historically two significant Marys who were the mothers of two special Jesus-individualities—one of which became the saviour of the world, Christ-Jesus.

Moreover, since the Holy Spirit (the Divine Sophia)—as the feminine-person of God—exists as pure virginal substance prior to divine inception, and expansive maternal procreation after divine inception, each of the two Marys is especially imbued with one of these two existential-states of the Holy Spirit. The Blessed Virgin Mary is superlatively imbued with the ever-youthful, immaculate *virginal* forces of the Holy Spirit-Sophia; while the Blessed Mother Mary is superlatively imbued with the propagative, nurturing *maternal* forces of the Holy Spirit-Sophia.

NOTES

CHAPTER 2

1. At certain developmental stages and in certain psychological conditions, human beings don't fully manifest self-conscious awareness: such as with unborn babies and young infants; and during sleep or in a coma. This is not to suggest that human beings at these stages or in these conditions are not persons.

    Esoterically understood, in all four instances the astral body and ego (self-consciousness) are partially or temporarily outside the physical body. In spite of diminished self-awareness, these human beings still possess an individualized ego and are therefore regarded as persons.
2. Most businesses today have a unique "logo," which is a simple and concise symbol, design or trademark that visually identifies the company. Rather amazingly, in the case of the "I am" word-symbol as a logo for self-awareness, even though it is the same logo for everyone, it can also uniquely apply to each individual person. In other words, my "I am" is unique to me, and distinct from your "I am," which is unique to you.

NOTES

CHAPTER 3

3. Within human experience, there is the comparable (though much more mundane) psychological aspect commonly known as "personality." The character of a person may be positively comprised of a number of different personalities (such as a "home" personality, a "work" personality or a "holiday" personality); but that does not mean that each personality is a different person. In this case, there is only *one* person, within which there exists various personalities.
4. Since the deific personification of supernal self-awareness is the perfect union of divine masculinity and divine femininity, the Eternal Son could also be more accurately designated "the Eternal Son-Daughter," or "the Eternal Child," or "the Eternal Offspring," or "the Eternal Progeny."
5. Since each divine-person has existed throughout eternity, any "before" and "after" relationship is understood to be a logical succession and not a chronological one. Logically, "self" and "knowing" must exist *before* "self-knowing" can exist; but in eternity there is no before and after in time—only the eternal NOW.
6. In Western theology, the divine-person of the Father singularly generates or eternally "begets" the divine-person of the Son; and together, the Father and the Son eternally conceive or "spirate" the divine-person of the Holy Spirit.
7. According to Western theology, it is the deep mutual love of the Father and the Son that eternally generates ("spirates") the Holy Spirit. As explained by John Paul II in a General Audience (November 20, 1985):

> The Father who begets loves the Son who is begotten. The Son loves the Father with a love which is identical with that of the Father. In the unity of the

divinity, love is on one side paternal and on the other, filial. At the same time the Father and the Son are not only united by that mutual love as two Persons infinitely perfect. But their mutual gratification, their reciprocal love, proceeds in them and from them as a person. The Father and the Son "spirate" the Spirit of Love consubstantially with them. In this way God, in the absolute unity of the divinity, is from all eternity Father, Son and Holy Spirit.

CHAPTER 4

8. A somewhat similar deific triplicity occurs in the Hindu Trimurti of Brahma, Vishnu and Shiva. In this case, the one god, Brahman, appears or manifests as Brahma when he is creating, as Vishnu when he is preserving, and as Shiva when he is destroying. Unlike the Divine Trinity, Brahma, Vishnu and Shiva are not distinct divine-persons, but simply three functional-forms of Brahman.

CHAPTER 5

9. For a more detailed and thorough study of the Logos-Word, the interested reader is referred to a previous publication by this author entitled *The Divine Trinity, the Logos-Word and Creation* (2015) which is available from Amazon.com.

CHAPTER 6

10. According to spiritual science, Ahriman is a powerful supernatural being who is tenaciously opposed to the progressive, divinely-instituted destiny of mankind and

the earth. Ahriman is also known by several other names, such as: Satan, Mephistopheles, the Devil, the Great Red Dragon, the spirit of darkness, and the unlawful prince of this world. Moreover, unlike Western theology, Ahriman is esoterically regarded as a being separate and distinct from the supernatural being known as Lucifer. For more detailed information regarding Ahriman, the interested reader is referred to *From Darkness to Light: Divine Love and the Transmutation of Evil* (2016) by this author, and available from Amazon.com.

11. On the pedestal of a statue of Isis in Sais, Egypt, was written the following inscription: "I am what was, what is and what shall be. No mortal has yet lifted my veil."

CHAPTER 7

12. According to spiritual science, the Lemurian Age existed millions of years ago at a time when the molten, magmatic surface of the earth began cooling sufficiently to form solid, habitable land masses. It was during the extensive Lemurian Age that human life-forms were gifted with the first faint spark of self-conscious awareness.

13. Since Lucifer, as attested to in Genesis, has long been allegorically visualized as a great serpent, the figure of Typhon is an apt mythological representation. As described by Nonnus of Panopolis (c.5th century) in *Dionysiaca*, Typhon was a:

> poison-spitting viper ... [whose] every hair belched viper-poison ... [who] spat out showers of poison from his throat ... the monster showered fountains from the viperish bristles of his high head ... [and] the water-snakes of the monster's viperish feet crawl into the caverns underground, spitting poison!

14. As expressed by Rudolf Steiner in a lecture given on 24 December 1924 entitled "Search for the New Isis, the Divine Sophia: The Quest for the Isis-Sophia":

> [T]he divine Sophia, the wisdom that enables us to see into the world with understanding ... We do not lack Christ; but the knowledge of Christ, the Sophia of Christ, the Isis of Christ is lacking.
>
> [W]hat we have lost is the knowledge of Christ Jesus, insight into his being. This is what we must find again with the power of the Jesus Christ who is in us.

15. During the Middle Ages, there were also a number of prominent, non-Christian intellectual thinkers such as Muslim philosopher, Ibn Rushd (Latin: "Averroës"; 1126–1198). Though Averroës has been credited with introducing Medieval Europe to Aristotelian philosophy, it was unfortunately a distorted version that St. Thomas Aquinas was forced to correct. Moreover, many of Averroës' philosophical assertions were contrary to Christian belief.
16. A more thorough analysis of ancient Gnosticism from an esoteric-Christian perspective is included in this author's earlier publication: *The Son of Love and the Birth of the New Mysteries* (2014), available from Amazon.com.

CHAPTER 8

17. According to spiritual science, the Archangel Michael has advanced to the next highest level of cosmic evolution, and is now able to function as a "principality" (also known as an "archai" or "time spirit").
18. In the words of Rudolf Steiner:

> Christ will appear again in his spiritual form during

the course of the twentieth century, not through the arrival of external events alone, but because human beings find the power represented by the holy Sophia. (From a lecture given on 24 December 1924 entitled "Search for the New Isis, the Divine Sophia: The Quest for the Isis-Sophia")

19. Briefly summarized, anthroposophical "spiritual science" is an independent esoteric-Christian offshoot of the Rosicrucian Fraternity that was established in the early-twentieth century by Austrian philosopher and esotericist, Rudolf Steiner (1861–1925). In accordance with its scientific character, anthroposophical spiritual science does not rely on divine revelation or pre-established dogma for supernatural information; but instead, trained supersensible perception is directed to the spiritual world in a fully-conscious, intellectual manner in order to objectively establish verifiable spiritual truth.

CHAPTER 9

20. According to the clairvoyant investigations of Levi H. Dowling (1844–1911), access to the akashic records is supersensibly guarded by an advanced spirit of wisdom named Visel. As stated in the *Aquarian Gospel*:

> "Behold the Akasha! Behold the Record Galleries of Visel where every thought and word and deed of every living thing is written down.
>
> I breathe upon you now the Holy Breath; you will discriminate, and you will know the lessons that these Record Books of God are keeping now for men of this new age.
>
> This age will be an age of splendour and of light,

because it is the home age of the Holy Breath; and the Holy Breath will testify anew for Christ, the Logos of eternal Love."

CHAPTER 10

21. All created beings reflect the Divine Trinity to greater or lesser degrees; and therefore each is a balance of masculine and feminine forces. Yahweh-Elohim, the exalted spirit of the moon, then, is no exception. Unfortunately, throughout the Old Testament, Yahweh-Elohim was depicted almost entirely as a stern, authoritative, masculine deity; even though the mission of this celestial-being was to apply the moon-forces of heredity and propagation in order to generate an appropriate physical body from amongst the Hebrew people for the incarnation of the Messiah

    In many other ancient cultures, the spirit of the moon was recognized as feminine: such as Phoebe, Artemis and Selene among the ancient Greeks; and Luna and Diana among the ancient Romans.

22. As described by Rudolf Steiner in *Occult Science* (2011):

    > [In ancient times] the relationships of reproduction remained outside the horizon of man's consciousness, and were subject to the guidance of the spiritual world. Whenever a soul had to descend into the Earth sphere, the impulses for reproduction arose in man on Earth. For Earthly consciousness the whole process was veiled to some extent in mystery and darkness.

23. A bodhisattva is a highly-advanced being who selflessly renounces the attainment of superphysical buddhahood in order to physically incarnate out of compassion to help

NOTES

others.

24. For a much more detailed account of these events, the interested reader is referred to this author's previous publication entitled *The Star of Higher Knowledge: The Five Guiding Mysteries of Esoteric Christianity* (2015).
25. On pages 40 and 41 of the National Geographic magazine's December 2015 edition—which headlined Mary—a diagrammatic timeline from 1531 to the present is given that dramatically illustrates the exponential increase in reported Marian apparitions since 1900.

CHAPTER 11

26. "Virginity," as it esoterically applies to both Marys, obviously means something much more profound than simply "sexual chastity."

CHAPTER 12

27. In the following statement that Rudolf Steiner made in a lecture given on May 1908 entitled "The Nature of the Virgin Sophia and of the Holy Spirit," he makes it very clear that spiritual science doesn't focus on the "coming of Sophia" in the sixth post-Atlantean cultural era, but on the "second coming of Christ":

> This is the cosmic, historical significance of spiritual science. It is to prepare humankind and to keep its eyes open for the time when Christ will come again among human beings in the sixth cultural epoch.

SELECT BIBLIOGRAPHY

(in alphabetical order)

- Blessed Anne Catherine Emmerich, *The Life of the Blessed Virgin Mary* (Aeterna Press, 2015)

- Boethius, *The Consolation of Philosophy* (Clarendon Press, 1999)

- Dante Alighieri, *Il Convivio* (Società editrice il Mulino, 1972)

- Dante Alighieri, *La Divina Commedia Di Dante Alighieri* (BiblioBazaar, 2008)

- Dietrich von Hildebrand, *Transformation in Christ: On the Christian Attitude* (Ignatius Press, 2001)

- Geoffrey Hodson, *The Brotherhood of Angels and of Men* (Ariel Press, 2011)

- G. R. S. Mead, *Pistis Sophia: A Gnostic Gospel* (Cambridge University Press, 2012)

SELECT BIBLIOGRAPHY

- Holy Bible, *RSV-CE* (Ignatius Press, 2006)

- Levi Dowling, *The Aquarian Gospel of Jesus the Christ* (Dover Publications, Inc., 2008)

- Ron MacFarlane, *From Darkness to Light: Divine Love and the Transmutation of Evil* (Greater Mysteries Publications, 2016)

- Ron MacFarlane, *The Greater Mysteries of the Divine Trinity, the Logos-Word and Creation* (Greater Mysteries Publications, 2015)

- Ron MacFarlane, *The Son of Love and the Birth of the New Mysteries* (Greater Mysteries Publications, 2014)

- Ron MacFarlane, *The Star of Higher Knowledge: The Five Guiding Mysteries of Esoteric Christianity* (Greater Mysteries Publications, 2015)

- Rudolf Steiner, *Isis Mary Sophia: Her Mission and Ours* (SteinerBooks, 2003)

- Rudolf Steiner, *Knowledge of the Higher Worlds and its Attainment* (Anthroposophic Press, Inc., 1986)

- Rudolf Steiner, *The Gospel of St. Luke* (Rudolf Steiner Press, 1988)

- Rudolf Steiner, *The Gospel of St. Matthew* (Rudolf Steiner Press, 1985)

- Samuel Zinner, *The Gospel of Thomas* (The Matherson Trust, 2011)

OTHER BOOKS BY

RON MACFARLANE

THERE IS a puzzling and pervasive misconception in present-day thinking that the existence of God cannot be intellectually determined, and that mentally accepting the existence of God is strictly a matter of non-rational belief (faith).

As such, contemplating God's existence is erroneously regarded as the exclusive subject of faith-based or speculative ideologies (religion and philosophy) which have no proper place in natural scientific study.

The fact is, there are a number of very convincing intellectual arguments concerning the existence of God that have been around for hundreds of years. Indeed, the existence of God can be determined with compelling intellectual certainty—provided the thinker honestly wishes to do so. Moreover, recent advances and discoveries in science have not weakened previous intellectual arguments for God's existence, but instead have enormously strengthened and supported them.

Intellectually assenting to the existence of God is easily demonstrated to be a superlatively logical conclusion, not some vague irrational conceptualization. Remarkably, at the present time there are only two seriously-competing intellectual explanations of life: the existence of God (the "God-hypothesis") and the existence of infinite universes (the "multiverse theory"). The postulation of an infinite number of unobservable universes is clearly a desperate attempt by atheistic scientists to avoid the God-hypothesis as the most credible and logical intellectual explanation of life and the universe. Moreover, under intellectual scrutiny, the scientifically celebrated "evolutionary theory" is here demonstrated to be fatally-flawed (philosophically illogical) as a credible explanation of life.

In this particular discourse, five well-known intellectual arguments for God's existence will be thoroughly examined. In considering these arguments, every attempt has been made to include current contributions, advances and discoveries that have modernized the more traditional arguments. Prior to examining these particular arguments for God, the universal predilection to establish intellectual 'oneness'—"monism"—will be considered in detail as well as the recurring propensity to postulate the existence of one supreme being—"monotheism."

Once intellectual certainty of one Supreme Being is established, a number of divine attributes can be logically deduced as well. Eleven of these attributes will be determined and examined in greater detail.

This book is available to order from Amazon.com

FOR COUNTLESS esoteric students today, the Mystery centres of ancient times have retained a powerful and fascinating allure. Moreover, there is often a wishful longing to revive and continue their secretive initiatory activity into modern times.

Unfortunately, this anachronistic longing is largely based on an illusionary misunderstanding of these Mysteries and the real reasons for their destined demise.

The primary reason for the disappearance of the ancient Mysteries is that they have been supplanted by the superior new mysteries—the mysteries of the Son. These new mysteries were initiated by Christ-Jesus himself. In order to better understand these Son-mysteries in a spiritually-scientific way, Rudolf Steiner (1861–1925) established the Anthroposophical Movement and Society.

Unfortunately, anthroposophy today has become unduly influenced by members and leaders who long to transform spiritual science into a modern-day Mystery institution. Moreover, contrary to his own words and intentions, Rudolf Steiner is even claimed to be the founder of some new "Michael-Mysteries."

By carefully establishing a correct esoteric understanding of the ancient pagan Mysteries, as well as a better appreciation of the new mysteries of the Son, this well-researched and readable discourse convincingly shows that all current and past attempts to revive the ancient pagan Mysteries regressively diverts human development backward to the seducer of mankind, Lucifer, rather than progressively forward to the saviour of mankind, Christ-Jesus.

Moreover, by additionally tracing the intriguing historical development of esoteric Christianity (particularly the Knights of the Holy Grail and Rosicrucianism) alongside Freemasonry, the Knights Templar and Theosophy, this important and necessary study illuminates the correct esoteric position and true significance of anthroposophical spiritual science.

This book is available to order from Amazon.com

THE PRIDE OF civilized mankind—intellectual thinking—is at a critical crossroads today. No doubt surprising to many, the cognitive capacity to consciously formulate abstract ideas in the mind, and then to manipulate them according to devised rules of logic in order to acquire new knowledge has only been humanly possible for about the last 3,000 years. Prior to intellectual (abstract) thinking, mental activity characteristically consisted of vivid pictorial images that arose spontaneously in the human mind from natural and supernatural stimuli.

The ability to think abstractly is the necessary foundation for mathematics, language and empirical science. The developmental history of intellectual thought, then, exactly parallels the developmental history of mathematics, language and science. Moreover, since abstract thinking inherently encourages the cognitive separation of subject (the thinker) and object (the perceived environment), the history of intellectual development also parallels the historical development of self-conscious (ego) awareness.

Over the last 3000 years, mankind in general has slowly perfected intellectual thinking; and thereby developed complex mathematics, sophisticated languages, comprehensively-detailed empirical sciences and pronounced ego-awareness. Unfortunately, all this intellectual activity over the many previous centuries has also exclusively strengthened human awareness of the physical, material world and substantially decreased awareness of the superphysical spiritual world.

That is why today, intellectual thinking is at a critical crossroads in further development. Thinking (intellectual or otherwise) is a superphysical activity—an activity within the soul. Empirical science is incorrect in postulating that physical brain tissue generates thought. The brain is simply the biological "sending and receiving" apparatus: sending sense-perceptions to the soul and receiving thought-conceptions from the soul. All this activity certainly generates chemical and electrical activity within the brain; but this activity is the effect, not the cause of thinking.

The danger to future intellectual thought is that increased acceptance of the erroneous scientific notion that thinking is simply brain-chemistry will increasingly deny and deaden true superphysical thinking. Future thinking runs the risk of becoming "a self-fulfilled prophecy"—the more people fervently believe that thought is simply brain-chemistry, the more thought will indeed become simply brain-chemistry. As a result, future human beings will be less responsible for generating their own thinking activity and more involuntarily controlled by their own brain chemistry. The artificial intelligence of machines won't become more human; but instead human beings will become more like robotic machines.

Presently, then, empirical science is leading intellectual thinking in a downward, materialistic direction. Correspondingly, however, true spiritual science (anthroposophy) is also actively engaged in leading intellectual thought back to its superphysical source in the soul. *Physical Science to Spiritual Science: the Future Development of Intellectual Thought* begins by examining the historical development of intellectual thinking and the corresponding rise of physical science. Once this has been discussed, practical and detailed information is presented on how spiritual science is leading intellectual thinking back to its true soul-source. It is intended that upon completion of this discourse, sincere and open-minded readers will themselves come to experience the exhilarating, superphysical nature of their own intellectual thought.

This book is available to order from Amazon.com

THE DIVINE TRINITY—the greatest of all Christian mysteries. How is it that the one God is a unity of three divine persons? Christ-Jesus first revealed this mystery to his disciples when on earth. Later, around the sixth century, the Trinitarian mystery was theologically clarified and outlined by the formulation of the Athanasian Creed.

Conceptual understanding of the divine Trinity has changed very little in Western society since then. Similarly with the theological understanding of the Logos-Word, as mentioned in the Gospel of St. John. The traditional understanding, that has remained essentially unchallenged for centuries, is that the Logos-Word is synonymous with God the Son. As for creation, the best that mainstream Christianity has historically provided is an ancient, allegorical account contained in the Book of Genesis.

Out of the hidden well-springs of esoteric Christianity, and as the title indicates, *The Greater Mysteries of the Divine Trinity, the Logos-Word and Creation*, delves much more deeply into the profound mysteries of the Trinitarian God, the Logos-Word of St. John and the creation of the universe. The divine Trinity is here demonstrated to be the loving union of Heavenly Father, Holy Mother and Eternal Son. The Logos-Word is here evidenced to be the "Universal Man," the primordial cosmic creation of God the Son. Universal creation itself is here detailed to be the "one life becoming many"—the multiplication of the Logos-Word into countless individualized life-forms and beings.

OTHER BOOKS

The depth and breadth of original and thought-provoking information presented here will, no doubt, stimulate and excite those esoteric thinkers who are seriously seeking answers to the deeper mysteries of life, existence and the universe.

> This book is available to order from Amazon.com

WHEN CHRIST-JESUS walked the earth over two thousand years ago, he established a two-fold division in his teaching that has continued to this day. To the general public, he simplified his teaching and presented it in pictorial, allegorical and figurative imagery in the form of stories, parables and lessons that could be imaginatively and intuitively understood.

To his inner circle of disciples (who were sufficiently prepared), however, he taught intellectual concepts, clear ideas and logical reasoning that could be understood on a much deeper and wider level of comprehension. As biblically explained:

> Then the disciples came and said to him, "Why do you speak to them [the general public] in parables?" And he answered them, "To you it has been given to know the secrets of the kingdom of heaven, but to them it has not been given ... This is why I speak to them in parables, because seeing they do not see, and hearing they do not hear, nor do they understand." (Matt 13:10, 13)

Moreover, in union with the divine, Our Saviour was able to reveal sacred knowledge that had never been previously presented in the entire history of mankind: "I will explain mysteries hidden since the creation of the world" (Matt 13:35). This sacred and revealed knowledge has been termed "Christ-mysteries" or "mysteries of the Son."

After his glorious resurrection and ascension, Christ-Jesus

institutionalized his two-fold mystery-teachings through St. Peter and St. John (the evangelist, not the apostle). Through St. Peter, Our Saviour instituted a universal Christian *religion* and *theology* to preserve, promote and convey the more basic and simplified mystery-teachings that are intended for the general public. Through St. John, Christ-Jesus instituted a universal Christian *philosophy* and *theosophy* to preserve, promote and convey the more comprehensive and complex mystery-teachings that are intended for the more advanced disciples (Christian initiates). In esoteric terminology, the institutionalized teachings through St. Peter are known as the "lesser mysteries of exoteric Christianity." The institutionalized teachings through St. John are known as the "greater mysteries of esoteric Christianity."

While both mystery-teaching approaches are equally sacred, profound and intended to complement each other, corrupt and intolerant authorities within the universal institution (Church) of St. Peter, for many centuries, persecuted and attacked any public expressions of esoteric Christianity. Consequently, genuine historical forms of esoteric Christianity, such as the Knights of the Holy Grail and the Fraternity of the Rose-Cross, were forced to be secretive and publically-hidden during the past two thousand years.

Thankfully today, the social, political and intellectual climate has progressed to the point where the greater mystery-teachings of esoteric Christianity can begin to be publically revealed for the first time. This modern-day outpouring really began with the twentieth-century establishment of anthroposophy by Rudolf Steiner (1861–1925). The information and approach presented in *The Star of Higher Knowledge: The Five Guiding Mysteries of Esoteric Christianity* is intended to augment and continue the mystery-teachings of Christ-Jesus as safeguarded by the Rosicrucian Fraternity and publicized through anthroposophy.

Consequently, this particular discourse delves much more deeply and comprehensively into the cosmos-changing salvational achievement of Christ-Jesus: the historical and cosmic preparations; as well as his birth, life, death, resurrection and ascension. While much of this mystery information may be unfamiliar, unknown and unexpected to mainstream (exoteric) Christianity, it in no way is meant to criticize, denigrate or displace the profound teachings of the universal Church; but rather, to complement, to enhance and to enlarge—for the betterment of true Christianity and, thereby, the betterment of all mankind.

This book is available to order from Amazon.com

OTHER BOOKS

Also check out the authour's website:

www.heartofshambhala.com

A Site Dedicated to True Esoteric Christianity

Contemporary Christianity, the world religion established by the God-Man, Christ-Jesus, and founded on the revelatory-principle that "God is love," is hardly the shining example of ideological unity and universal brotherhood that it was intended to be. There are approximately 41,000 different Christian denominations in the world today, many of which are fervently hostile to each other.

Atheistic and anti-Christian polemicists have concluded that there is something inherently wrong with Christianity itself and, in consequence, it is doomed to failure and eventual extinction.

Discerning Christian advocates, however, know that any apparent failure to realize the high ideals of Christianity is not due to the profound teachings and the illustrious life-example of Christ-Jesus, but instead to the limitations of wounded human nature. Corrupt, power-hungry, destructive and evil-minded human beings have twisted, distorted and fragmented true Christianity for the past two thousand years, and continue to do so today.

Moreover, on a much deeper spiritual level, since Christianity is indeed a divinely-initiated endeavor to help restore "fallen" humanity, powerful and demonic beings have attempted to destroy nascent Christianity from its very inception. But thankfully, according to Christ-Jesus himself, "the powers of hell will not prevail against it [Christianity]" (Matt 16:18).

Sadly contributing to the injurious fragmentation of Christianity—the "religion of divine love"—is the sectarian hostility between certain proponents of anthroposophy and select members of the Catholic Church. In both cases, this is largely due to ignorance; that is, an almost complete lack of understanding about the true significance and mission of the other—anthroposophical critics know almost nothing of Catholicism, and Catholic critics know almost nothing about anthroposophy.

The wonderful reconciliatory fact is that anthroposophy and Catholicism are not conflicting polar opposites, but are instead like two sides of the same golden coin—different, but complementary. Instead of only one side or the other being the only true approach to Christ-Jesus, both are uniquely necessary and both positively contribute to the complete truth of Christianity.

Since this author is happily and harmoniously both an anthroposophist and a Catholic, *The Greater and Lesser Mysteries of Christianity: The Complementary Paths of Anthroposophy and Catholicism* earnestly seeks to correct the misinformation and lack of understanding that each partisan critic has for the other. As in almost every significant dispute, increased knowledge and familiarity about each other will in time bring both sides closer together for mutual growth and benefit.

This book is available to order from Amazon.com

MARY AND THE DIVINE SOPHIA

IN THE LIGHT of spiritual science, never before in the history of the world has there been such an assailment of supernatural evil upon humanity as extensive and intense as there exists at the present time. Subconsciously pouring into the human soul are the seductive whisperings of Luciferic beings and fallen angels; the perceptual distortions of Ahrimanic (Satanic) beings; the lurid, egocentric promptings of corrupt spirits of personality (asuras); and the violent inducements of blood-lust rising up from the subterranean "beast of Revelation" (Sorath the sun-demon).

The tragic and bitter irony of all this, however, is that because of today's pervasive, atheistic and secular culture and the materialistic worldview of natural science, individual human beings are correspondingly the most oblivious to supernatural evil than they have ever been at any other time in world history.

To be sure, people today are certainly aware of the *effects* of supernatural evil—extensive and increased natural disasters; horrific instances of mass genocide; the prolific use of torture and brutality by government agencies; individual acts of sudden cruelty and murder; pathological selfishness throughout the world's business and financial markets; strange, globally-infectious viral contagions; the devaluation of human life through abortion and euthanasia; and a world-wide pandemic of dehumanizing drug addiction. What most people today fail to realize is that the invisible fomenting agents—the *causes*—of all these life-threatening, destructive physical events and pathologies are ultimately rooted in the impulses of supernatural evil.

To be sure, mankind would have completely and totally

succumbed to this tsunami of supernatural evil if it weren't for the protective and opposing intervention of powerful, benevolent celestial beings, such as St. Michael the Archai, Yahweh-Elohim (the spirit of the moon), and the Solar-Christos (aka: "Christ"—the regent of the sun).

More than ever, it is crucially important in today's world to understand the nature of evil, and to become more aware and cognizant of the various perpetrators of supernatural evil. Thereby, conscious cooperation with the compassionate protectors and guardians of mankind can be increased and strengthened, so that supernatural evil is better resisted and eventually overcome.

To this end, *From Darkness to Light: Divine Love and the Transmutation of Evil* delves deeply into the thorny questions of "What exactly is evil?", together with "How and when did evil begin?", as well as "Why does God allow evil to exist?" Once the nature, genesis and purpose of evil is better understood, then various influential superphysical perpetrators of supernatural evil will be examined in closer detail. Correspondingly, the superphysical proponents of cosmic holiness will be identified and better understood as well.

Wherever possible, the spiritual-scientific research of anthroposophy—an independent offshoot of the Rosicrucian Fraternity, and the modern-day expression of esoteric Christianity that was established by Rudolf Steiner (1861–1925)—will be included and referenced. Following this profoundly-esoteric background, the destined human struggle with continuing and obdurate evil—far into the future development of the earth—will also be mentally envisioned and supersensibly examined.

It is sincerely intended that upon completion of the entire written discourse, concerned individuals will be better armed and shielded in order to become actively engaged on the side of holiness and spiritual light in the prolonged cosmic battle against evil and material darkness.

This book is available to order from Amazon.com

www.ingramcontent.com/pod-product-compliance
Lightning Source LLC
Chambersburg PA
CBHW031942070426
42450CB00006BA/731